P9-CKR-869

Encountering
the Chinese

The InterAct Series
GEORGE W. RENWICK, *Series Editor*

Encountering the Chinese

A Guide for Americans

SECOND EDITION

HU WENZHONG and
CORNELIUS L. GROVE

INTERCULTURAL PRESS, INC.

First published by Intercultural Press. For information, contact:

Intercultural Press, Inc.
PO Box 700
Yarmouth, Maine 04096, USA
207-846-5168
Fax: 207-846-5181
www.interculturalpress.com

Nicholas Brealey Publishing
36 John Street
London, WC1N 2AT, UK
44-207-430-0224
Fax: 44-207-404-8311
www.nbrealey-books.com

© 1991, 1999 by Hu Wenzhong and Cornelius L. Grove

All rights reserved. No part of this publication may be reproduced in any manner whatsoever without written permission from the publisher, except in the case of brief quotations embodied in critical articles or reviews.

Printed in the United States of America

05   04   03   02   01   3   4   5   6   7

Library of Congress Cataloging-in-Publication Data

Hu, Wenzhong, 1935–
    Encountering the Chinese: a guide for Americans/ Hu Wenzhong and Cornelius L. Grove— 2nd ed.
        p.   cm.
    Includes bibliographical references.
    ISBN 1-877864-58-7 (alk. paper)
    1. National characteristics, Chinese. 2. China—Social life and customs—1976– . I. Grove, Cornelius Lee. II. Title.
DS721.H71114   1999
306'.0951—dc21   98–39919
                                                  CIP

Table of Contents

WITHDRAWN

SHATFORD LIBRARY

SEP   2002

PASADENA CITY COLLEGE
1570 E. COLORADO BLVD
PASADENA, CA 91106

Part II—Advice for Americans Living and Working in the PRC

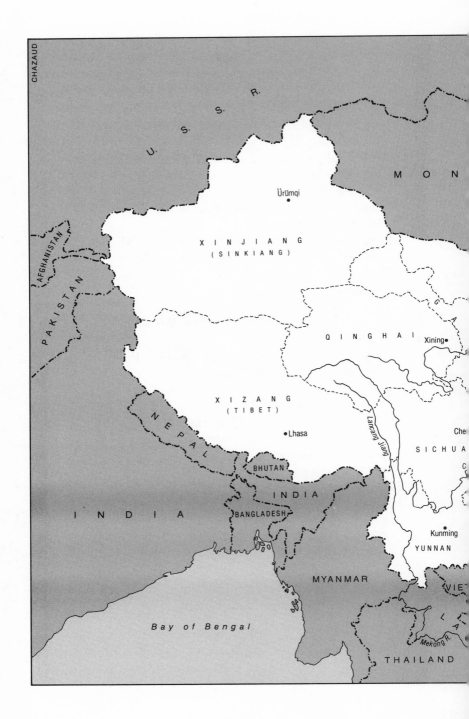

Acknowledgments

Between February and June 1986, Cornelius L. Grove traveled to the People's Republic of China (PRC) with the financial support of AFS Intercultural Programs and the Nathaniel Winthrop Foundation. He received additional support from Beijing Foreign Studies University, where he served as a visiting professor. Without support from these institutions, he would not have been able to go to China or to join his Chinese co-author in carrying out the preliminary discussions and planning that led to this handbook.

From March 1988 to January 1989, Hu Wenzhong was in the United States, where he devoted much of his time to writing this book. He had support from the United Board for Christian Higher Education in Asia and from the Pennsylvania State University at Harrisburg, where he was a visiting professor. Without these institutional sources of support, he would not have been able to remain in the United States long enough to undertake the writing tasks required.

David S. Hoopes, editor-in-chief of Intercultural Press, strongly encouraged the authors to proceed with this project and offered thoughtful advice as the work proceeded.

Steven and Frances Grove of York Haven, Pennsylvania, and Robert and Edith Grove of Walnutport, Pennsylvania, generously made their homes and other resources available so that the authors could meet several times during the spring and summer of 1988.

Jan Carol Berris, Bob Geyer, Rebecca Karl, Stephanie Mitchell, Linda A. Reed, and Paul Schroeder—all of them highly experienced in the ways of the People's Republic of China—read the entire manuscript and offered detailed comments and suggestions that have contributed substantially to the accuracy and thoroughness of the information in this book. The unselfish commitment of time and energy by these "old China hands" did much to sustain the authors through the long hours of writing and rewriting.

Paul Feltman, Mary-Jean Hayden, Hu Chun, Deborah Leonard, Betty Lum, Sarah Judge McCalpin, and Marcia Miller—also very familiar with the People's Republic—read two or more chapters and provided detailed critiques. Their enthusiasm also was an important encouragement for the authors.

William Abnett, Douglas Murray, McKinney Russell, and Fred Wakeman—leading American authorities on China— read the entire manuscript in final draft and reassured the authors that the information it contained was fundamentally sound. The authors found the approval of these experts heartening.

When we revised this handbook in 1997–98, Kay M. Jones and Tony Pan offered well-informed advice and specific recommendations for changes and additions and wrote reviews of four recently published books for the Recommended Readings section. As consultants specializing in China, Kay and Tony have used Encountering the Chinese with their clients and trainees since its original publication; we knew we were lucky to have their generous input.

The institutions and individuals named above have the authors' gratitude. Their support, advice, and assistance will be long and fondly remembered. None of the institutions or individuals named above, however, can be held responsible for errors of omission or commission that may be found herein. Any shortcomings in the substance and content of this handbook are solely the responsibility of the authors.

—Hu Wenzhong
Cornelius L. Grove

The authors are grateful for permission to quote from the following:

From *Iron and Silk*, by Mark Salzman. New York: Random House, 1986, 36–37, 122–23. Copyright © 1986 Mark Salzman. Reprinted by permission of the publisher.

From "Social Orientation and Individual Modernity among Chinese Students in Taiwan," by Kuo-shu Yang. *Journal of Social Psychology* 113 (1981): 159–60. Copyright © 1981 Helen Dwight Reid Educational Foundation. Reprinted by permission of Heldref Publications.

From "The China Trade: Making the Deal," by Lucian W. Pye. *Harvard Business Review* 64, no. 4 July-August 1986, 79. Copyright © 1986 President and Fellows of Harvard College; all rights reserved. Reprinted by permission of the publisher.

From "Chinese Values and the Search for Culture-Free Dimensions of Culture," by The Chinese Culture Connection. *Journal of Cross-Cultural Psychology* 18, no. 2, 147–48. Copyright © 1987 Western Washington University. Reprinted by permission of Sage Publications, Inc.

From *Chinese Reflections: Americans Teaching in the People's Republic*, by Tani E. Barlow and Donald M. Lowe. New York: Praeger Publishers, 1985, 82–83, 151, 152. Copyright © 1985 Praeger Publishers. Reprinted by permission of Greenwood Publishing Group, Inc., Westport, CT.

From *Law without Lawyers: A Comparative View of Law in China and the United States*, by Victor H. Li. Boulder, CO: Westview Press, 1978. Copyright © 1978 Westview Press. Reprinted by permission of Westview Press, a member of Perseus Books, L.L.C.

From "The Psychology of Chinese Organizational Behavior," by Gordon Redding and Gilbert Y. Y. Wong. *The Psychology of the Chinese People*, edited by Michael Harris Bond. New York: Oxford University Press. 1986, 288–89. Copyright © 1986 Oxford University Press. Reprinted by permission of the publisher.

Preface

Events occurring in U.S.-China relations and within China since 1991, the year the first edition of *Encountering the Chinese* was published, prompted Professor Hu and Dr. Grove to revise their already significant contribution to American understanding of Chinese culture. We sincerely thank them for this revision for two reasons. The first is that we have long recommended their book to complement our efforts in increasing cultural understanding between Americans and Chinese people, and we are pleased to be able to continue doing so. The second reason is that because we work on a daily basis as a bicultural team ourselves, we deeply appreciate the effort that was required to create both the original work and this revision. Renewed collaboration between Hu Wenzhong and Cornelius Grove can only lead us all to a greater understanding of what helps Americans interact successfully with Chinese people.

Many of the revisions for this edition are updates, reflecting events that have taken place within China and in U.S.-China relations since 1991. More subtle but more meaningful revisions have been written with an eye to further developing and refining some of the concepts introduced in the first edition. Finally, this edition is revised to broaden its appeal by taking up a few more concerns of business and professional circles than the first edition, while continuing to address the questions of others in their encounters with Chinese people.

Since 1991 China has seen sustained economic growth as the country continues to follow the path of modernization, even with the passing of Deng Xiaoping early in 1997. When Zhu Rongji succeeded Li Peng as premier of the People's Republic in 1998, Zhu reaffirmed the modernization policy and launched a program to reform state enterprises. U.S.-China relations have been enhanced by reciprocal state visits: President Jiang Zemin's state visit to the United States in 1997 and President Clinton's visit to China in 1998. On the international trade front, most multinationals are now engaged in business with China. Motorola, Boeing, Kodak, and McDonald's are becoming "household names" in China. Michael Jordan is known by Chinese grandmothers and teenagers alike.

Within this climate of diplomatic exchange and economic vitality, contacts and exchanges between Americans and Chinese have become increasingly frequent and even commonplace in business, academic, scientific, professional, personal, and cultural arenas. As contacts and exchanges increase, we hope that interactions will be positive, fruitful experiences for all parties. To this end, Encountering the Chinese helps Americans understand how to build better relationships with Chinese people by explaining the foundations of Chinese thinking and behavior. It offers specific guidelines for building mutual understanding and for developing solid professional and personal relationships. Although written specifically for those from the United States, this book should also be useful for other Westerners, particularly Canadians, Australians, and northern Europeans.

When bringing Americans together with Chinese counterparts, we have noticed that one of the first questions asked by Americans often concerns the dos and don'ts of interacting with Chinese people. These are covered in Encountering the

Chinese with more detail and practicality than in any other current publication of which we have knowledge. The second question that Americans usually bring up is how to overcome the language barrier. One way to do this is to learn some key vocabulary words and phrases in Mandarin. The Chinese greetings, terms, titles, and forms of address presented in this book will provide a base for beginning to build rapport with Chinese people. Overall, the best aspect of *Encountering the Chinese* is that it "systematically and thoroughly explains the values, habits of thought, and patterns of behavior of the Chinese," as Jan Carol Berris pointed out in the preface to the first edition.

Ms. Berris also stated that "the knowledge that can be gained from *Encountering the Chinese* provides Americans with the cement to hold together and strengthen their relationships" with Chinese people. We agree.

—Anthony Pan
Kay M. Jones
Belmont, CA
August 1998

Introduction to the Second Edition

Encountering the Chinese was originally completed during the summer of 1988. Although the framework of Chinese culture remains the same, significant changes necessitate this revision.

China's GNP has been growing at an annual rate of about 10 percent; economically, China has become one of the most exciting places in the world. Millions of peasants have left the land and moved into cities large and small. They have become workers in manufacturing, construction, service, and other industries.

Another big change is that overseas investment has been accelerating. Foreign investment is pouring into the PRC at the rate of about thirty billion dollars per annum, and foreign-owned companies and joint-venture enterprises have sprung up everywhere, especially in the coastal areas. China's export and import capacity has grown significantly, and its foreign currency reserves amounted in late 1997 to 120 billion dollars.

Socialist market economy reforms and foreign competition have forced a large number of state-owned companies into bankruptcy, and many workers have had to be retrained in order to find new jobs. The "iron rice bowl"—the promise of a job of *some* kind for every citizen—in many cases has become a "porcelain" one, and the differentials in pay have become larger. Millionaires number in the hundreds of thousands, while innumerable Chinese families still earn but a few hundred yuan a month.

Traditional values by and large remain the same, although one can notice a gradual shift in social norms and customs. China remains collectivist in nature, but individualism has been on the rise, especially among the young.

These changes have attracted ever larger numbers of foreigners to live, work, study, and teach in China. In order to better aid their adaptation, we have revised portions of our book. At the same time, we are gratified to find that while certain details required adjusting, most of what we wrote in 1988 about the basic values of the Chinese remains accurate.

Introduction to the First Edition

Encountering the Chinese is a practical guide for individuals from the United States who are involved in, or will be involved in, sustained face-to-face contacts with individuals from the People's Republic of China. This book should prove helpful for Americans who are establishing professional or personal relationships with citizens of the People's Republic anywhere in the world. Diplomats, "foreign experts," businesspeople, consultants, researchers, teachers, students, and community leaders who have extensive dealings with the Chinese will find this handbook useful. People who are traveling within China and who are eager to get to know Chinese people in more than a superficial way will also find guidance herein.

Anyone who is planning to interact with the Chinese in the People's Republic or elsewhere should know that a surprising number of Chinese people speak English. Many speak it remarkably well. Even though you may know little of Mandarin or any other Chinese dialect, you can count on communicating verbally with many of the Chinese whom you encounter. Approximately fifty Mandarin terms are included in the text (in *pinyin*, a system of romanized spelling); these are printed with appropriate tone graphs in the glossary. But this book is not about the Chinese language. It is about

Chinese culture, values, and patterns of life, the things you will need to understand if you are to have good personal relations with your Chinese associates.

One of the authors is from the People's Republic of China and one is from the United States of America. Each has lived and worked in the other's country, and each has read widely in the anthropological and sociological literature on his own culture as well as the other's. Both have talked at length with others who have crossed the cultural divide between the United States and the People's Republic. Both are familiar with the literature that deals with human contact across cultures and have themselves crossed other cultural divides as well.

We know that many Americans who live and work in China have a variety of interpersonal difficulties with their hosts. We know, too, that Americans who come into sustained contact with the Chinese in other nations encounter similar difficulties. We are convinced that those difficulties often arise out of the differences between the two value systems and cultures. These differences can be observed and described rather easily, and the types of problems they lead to are relatively well understood. In the following pages we will describe many of those differences and will try not only to make them understandable but also to suggest appropriate and productive responses to them.

Our principal objective in *Encountering the Chinese* is to describe significant patterns in the behavior of Chinese whose native country is the PRC.* We draw comparisons between Chinese and American behavior and attempt to interpret the reasons for the major differences between the two patterns. Such interpretations are at the cultural level and employ

---

* Some of our generalizations regarding the culture of the PRC also apply to the cultures of ethnic Chinese people who live in, or who emigrated from, other places in Asia such as Taiwan, Hong Kong, Singapore, Thailand, and Vietnam.

generalizations that are widely accepted by cross-cultural experts regarding the assumptions, values, habits of thought, and patterns of behavior considered characteristic of Chinese and American people.

These generalized interpretations obviously cannot hold the precise answer to a practical difficulty you may be facing in your encounters with citizens of the PRC. So you must be willing to apply our generalizations to whatever extent you can in order to increase your understanding of the people, events, behaviors, and emotions with which you are grappling.

If you are from a Western nation other than the United States, you are also likely to find this handbook useful. But we address ourselves to the American reader; we compare and contrast Chinese culture only with American culture. If you are not from the United States, it will be helpful if you are more or less familiar with American culture.

Chapter 1 provides important background information about the Chinese way of life and the Chinese value system. You should read this chapter first, even if you plan to read other material in parts I and II selectively or out of order.

Part I comprises chapters 2 through 10; it offers information and advice for Americans located anywhere in the world (including the People's Republic of China) who are interacting with the Chinese.

Part II offers information and advice that applies specifically to the People's Republic of China. It is intended for Americans and other Westerners who are, or soon will be, living and working (or studying) in that nation.

1

A Brief Background to the Chinese Way of Life

Group Cohesiveness in Contemporary China

China is the only country with a civilization stretching back continuously some five thousand years. Chinese civilization was built on agriculture; generations of peasants were tied to the land on which they lived and worked. Except in times of war and famine, there was very little mobility, either socially or geographically.

The agrarian nature of ancient Chinese society accounts for the cultural traits and values that came to characterize that society and that still characterize it today. Peasant families were cohesive units in which all members joined in the work of planting, raising, and harvesting. Often the entire population of a village was a clan or family group. Thus, family and clan membership was a key element in each peasant's identity. The collective (group-oriented) nature of Chinese values is largely the product of thousands of years of living and working together on the land.

The principal cohesive groups (primary groups) within Chinese society today are family, school, work unit, and local community. The daily life of virtually every Chinese is deeply embedded in his or her relationships with the other people in these groups. Very few significant relationships occur beyond the boundaries of these primary groups.

At first glance the relationships within a Chinese family may seem similar to those within an American family. But closer observation reveals important differences. Chinese parents are highly protective of their children. Even grown children depend on their parents' financial support until they find employment; they live in their parents' household until they are married, if not longer. Chinese children, even as adolescents, do not expect to earn their own money by means of part-time jobs and make no important decisions about their own daily comings and goings. Filial piety is one of the principal virtues counseled by Confucius; this virtue is not an abstraction but one that continues to be played out on a daily basis as children—including adult sons and daughters—demonstrate again and again that they are obedient to parents and solicitous of their welfare.

Extended families in China are remarkably cohesive. Geographical mobility is low, so the vast majority of Chinese live close to their siblings, parents, grandparents, aunts and uncles, cousins, and other relatives. Households that include three generations, though rapidly disappearing (especially in urban areas), are still far more common in China than in the United States. Family-centered values and physical closeness combine to ensure that most Chinese have relationships with the members of their extended families that are durable and that involve frequent instances of aid and support given and received.

In school at any level, Chinese students are enmeshed in another important network—that of peers. It is true that in the United States peer relationships among young people are intense, too, but there is an important difference. In China, schoolchildren remain members of the same small group of students not only during each school day and year but also during all the years they attend a particular school. Called the "class collective" and numbering anywhere from fifteen to fifty students, this group constitutes a strong force for stability and conformity. The class monitor, who is the leader of the class collective, bears responsibilities much broader than those of a class president in the United States. The class collective attends classes together, organizes other study activities, and participates as a unit in extracurricular activities such as intramural sports.

Every Chinese student belongs to a class collective; joining is not a matter of personal choice. Nor does one have a choice as to which collective he or she will join. Students are assigned to collectives by school administrators on the basis of similarity of academic programs. A student who remains apart from the activities of his or her collective is looked upon by peers as antisocial and quite odd. Members of the class are expected to take care of each other when misfortune strikes as well as to help each other in more ordinary ways. In spirit, a Chinese class collective is similar to an American sorority or fraternity. Relationships among Chinese classmates (especially those of the same sex) usually last indefinitely, becoming incorporated into each student's lifelong network of trusted friends.

Regardless of occupation or profession, most urban Chinese belong to a work unit, or *danwei*.* Strictly speaking, a danwei refers to a government office or an institution. But its use includes state-owned companies, factories and shops, hospitals, and universities and schools. Thus, independent entrepreneurs as well as Chinese who work in foreign-owned or joint-venture companies are generally not classified as belonging to a danwei. A Chinese danwei is quite different from employing organizations in the West. A work unit in China assigns productive tasks and pays wages, but it also administers all government regulations and policies that re-

---

* For guidance in pronouncing Chinese words, see Appendix A.

late to its workers and their families and has responsibility for a variety of other aspects of the lives of its members. For instance, the work unit is responsible for seeing that each worker's family is housed adequately. A large percentage of the Chinese population lives in housing (usually apartments) owned by the work unit; when such housing is unavailable, it is the work unit's responsibility to help its members find something suitable. Larger work units typically own and operate a medical clinic as well as a day-care center and a kindergarten; the largest ones also include primary and secondary schools. Family disputes are occasionally brought before the leaders of a work unit for arbitration.

Picnics, weekend outings, and other forms of recreation are typically organized by work unit administrators for workers and their family members. Large work units may arrange for their employees to vacation at a summer resort. Some financially secure work units even own and operate hostels at famous resorts such as Beidaihe. When an employee or a member of his or her family is ill or injured, the work unit makes sure that medical care is provided. When employees retire, the work unit gives them gifts during the Spring Festival. Finally, when a worker dies, the work unit helps with funeral arrangements and organizes memorial services. With the possible exception of a few successful company towns, there is no counterpart in the United States to the Chinese work unit.

The Chinese sometimes complain about their work units. An American might speculate that the complaints arise because work units tend to interfere too much in people's daily lives. On the contrary, the complaints most often arise because a work unit has not taken sufficient care of someone (for instance, has not provided that person with adequate housing) or has been unfair (for example, has seemed biased in its selection of members to go abroad). Most Chinese workers appreciate the close, nurturing atmosphere of the work unit as much as they do the caring and loving atmosphere of their families.

The neighborhood is another relatively close social unit. (In some cases it is difficult to differentiate clearly between the work unit and the neighborhood, since workers often live in apartments located on the grounds of their work unit.) The great majority of the Chinese live in crowded conditions and interact frequently with neighbors. They are likely to share the same courtyard and hallway, and in older buildings they may share a common bathroom and kitchen. Even when housing is less crowded, as in rural areas, the relationship between neighbors remains close. If a family dispute erupts, neighbors are likely to come in to mediate. In cities, neighborhood committees find jobs for unemployed people and try to patch up severely strained family relationships. The type of connectedness typical of Chinese neighborhoods would be viewed by the great majority of Americans as encroaching upon their personal prerogatives and privacy.

Before briefly discussing Chinese values, we should note that what we are calling Chinese society is in actuality the society of the Han, the dominant ethnic group in China. More than 90 percent of the Chinese are Han people. Nevertheless, there are several dozen other ethnic groups in the PRC such as Zhuangs, Mongolians, Tibetans, Uighurs, and Miaos. These national and ethnic minorities tend to cluster in either southwest or northwest China; few are found in the major eastern cities.

Three Fundamental Values of the Chinese

Collectivism is the term used by anthropologists and sociologists to designate one of the basic orientations of Chinese culture. This term should be thought of as located at one end of a continuum; at the other end is one of the basic orientations of U.S. culture, *individualism*.[1]

Individualism is not a term that describes something unique about American culture, but a set of assumptions and values that can be applied to a greater or lesser extent to many cultures, particularly those of Europe, Canada, the United States, Australia, and New Zealand. Likewise, collectivism is a term that more or less applies to many cultures, especially those in Asia, Africa, South America, Central America, and the Pacific Islands. Thus, while collectivism is not unique to China, it is clearly an integral part of China's culture. Here is how one group of scholars recently summarized the basic differences between individualism and collectivism.

Collectivism is characterized by individuals subordinating their personal goals to the goals of some collectives. Individualism is characterized by individuals subordinating the goals of collectives to their personal goals. A key belief of people in collectivist cultures is that the smallest unit of survival is the collective. A key belief of people in individualistic cultures is that the smallest unit of survival is the individual. In many situations people in collectivist cultures have internalized the norms of their collectives so completely that there is no such thing as a distinction between in-group goals and personal goals.[2]

Though collectivism originated in the agrarian economy of ancient China and in the ethics of Confucius, a few of the forms taken by contemporary Chinese collectivism are attributable to China's present political system. For example, the enveloping nature of the Chinese work unit is largely a product of that system. Another example is the relationship among neighbors. Though neighbors in China have traditionally been highly interdependent, the type of neighborhood committee that is an institutionalized provider of social services and mutual aid is quite new. In these and other ways, the tradition of collectivism has been enhanced since the founding of the People's Republic of China.

On the other hand, the burgeoning business economy of China's large cities, where Western influence is especially strong, is beginning to erode the ethic of collectivism. Western businesspeople frequently complain about the job-hopping of their Chinese employees and question how this is compatible with China's ancient collectivist ethic. The answer: it isn't. Job-hopping demonstrates individualistic values gaining a foothold in China.

Large power distance is another term from cross-cultural research that is useful in explaining Chinese values. Power distance indicates the extent to which the people in a society accept the fact that power in institutions and organizations is distributed unequally among individuals. Large power distance characterizes a society in which people are comfortable with an unequal distribution of power and thus do not try to bring about a more nearly equal distribution.[3]

Throughout their history the Chinese have shown respect for age, seniority, rank, maleness, and family background. Confucianism embodied this attitude toward power and authority by stressing the benefits of ordered hierarchical relationships. Over the past thirty or forty years in the PRC, however, the emphasis on socialist egalitarianism has noticeably eroded this way of thinking. In Chinese families the kind of absolute power wielded by the patriarch is a thing of the past.

Perhaps the chief determinant of relative power in China is seniority. Who is older and who is younger among siblings, for example, is of considerable importance. In Chinese, the age-neutral words *brother* and *sister* do not exist; instead, there are quite different words for older brother, younger brother, older sister, and younger sister. An elder sibling may call a younger one by his or her given name, but the younger one must use the more reverential age-relative title when addressing the older one—*gege* for elder brother and *jiejie* for elder sister. Similarly, age is important in local community affairs. What an older person says generally carries more weight in the meetings of the neighborhood committee than the opinions of younger people. Younger people are deferential to older ones, and informal but severe social sanctions may be applied toward anyone who is disrespectful to an elder neighbor.

In spite of recent attempts within Chinese institutions to promote more informal interaction among colleagues—such as, for example, encouraging the use of rank-free titles in everyday address—the force of tradition is so powerful that many young workers (those who might benefit most from such a change) cannot bring themselves to be anything but fully deferential toward their supervisors. Promotion is much more likely to be based on seniority than on outstanding performance. Cases can be found where able young people have been promoted over less able older colleagues, especially in foreign multinational companies operating in the PRC, but this circumstance is relatively rare and encounters resistance.

Family background is not as important as relative age but can be influential in certain matters. The criterion for a good family background has changed over time. Before 1949, someone whose father was wealthy was considered to be from a good background. But after the People's Republic was founded, those whose parents were workers, peasants, or "revolutionary cadres"[4] were said to have a good background. In recent years, the children of professors, scientists, and senior officials have made similar claims. Whatever the criterion, those from a good family are looked upon with favor in matters such as matrimony and job allocation.

Finally, the third important fundamental value of the Chinese is *intragroup harmony* and avoidance of overt conflict in interpersonal relations. People from cultures the world over value smooth human relationships, but the importance assigned to interpersonal harmony varies from one culture to another. With respect to the Chinese, maintaining harmonious relationships with family members, close friends and colleagues, and other primary group members is a matter of supreme concern. The disapproval of overt confrontation and the high value placed on intragroup harmony are themes that will occur again and again throughout this book.[5]

---

[1] Within the field of cross-cultural studies, the terms *collectivism* and *individualism* are most closely associated with Dutch researcher Geert Hofstede. See chapter 5 of his *Culture's Consequences: International Differences in Work-Related Values* (Newbury Park, CA: Sage, 1980), 213–60.

[2] Harry C. Triandis, Richard Brislin, and C. Harry Hui, "Cross-Cultural Training across the Individualism-Collectivism Divide," *International Journal of Intercultural Relations* 12, no. 3 (1988): 271.

[3] The terms *large power distance* and *small power distance* are most closely associated with Geert Hofstede. See chapter 3 of his *Culture's Consequences: International Differences in Work-Related Values* (Newbury Park, CA: Sage, 1980), 92–152.

[4] *Cadre*, often pronounced KAH-der by English-speaking Chinese and commonly used to refer to individuals (not a group, as in French), technically designates staff members of the Chinese government at all levels, including those in local work units. Its meaning is not unlike that of "bureaucrat." However, *cadre* is also used by the Chinese to refer to white-collar workers and people in positions of leadership in all walks of life. Service personnel are clearly not cadres, but different people have different ideas about the dividing line between cadre and noncadre. The Chinese term for cadre is *ganbu*.

[5] In the early 1980s, a group of social scientists from around the world conducted a survey of Chinese values. In order to avoid biasing the research by using Western values as their starting point—as has happened frequently in cross-cultural research—they approached a number of Chinese social scientists and asked them to prepare a list of at least ten "fundamental and basic values for Chinese people." This composite list appears in no particular order.

Filial piety
Tolerance of others
Humility
Observation of rites and
    social rituals
Kindness (forgiveness,
    compassion)

Wealth
Industry (working hard)
Harmony with others
Loyalty to superiors
Reciprocation of greetings, favors, and gifts

10

Moderation, following the middle way
Sense of righteousness
Benevolent authority
Personal steadiness and stability
Patriotism
Keeping oneself disinterested and pure
Patience
Sense of cultural superiority
Adaptability
Prudence (carefulness)
Having a sense of shame
Contentedness with one's position in life
Close, intimate friendship
Having few desires

Knowledge (education)
Solidarity with others
Self-cultivation
Ordering relationships by status and observing this order
Noncompetitiveness
Resistance to corruption
Sincerity
Thrift
Persistence (perseverance)
Repayment of both the good or the evil that another person has caused you
Trustworthiness
Courtesy
Being conservative
Protecting your "face"
Chastity in women
Respect for tradition

The Chinese Culture Connection, "Chinese Values and the Search for Culture-Free Dimensions of Culture," *Journal of Cross-Cultural Psychology* 18, no. 2 (June 1987), 143–64. (The Chinese Culture Connection is a multinational group of scholars headed by Michael Harris Bond of the Chinese University of Hong Kong.)

Part I:
Advice for Americans Interacting with the Chinese

In this part we offer information and advice for Americans located anywhere in the world (including the People's Republic of China) who are interacting with the Chinese.

2

Chinese Titles and Forms of Address

Chinese Naming Practices

In the United States a person's full name is written and spoken with the given name first and the family name second. In China the reverse is true: the family name is followed by the given name. In the Chinese name Zhang Minwen, for example, Zhang is the family name and Minwen is the given name. If an English title is added, the result would be Miss Zhang, Dr. Zhang, or Lieut. Zhang.

The Chinese who deal with Westerners sometimes reverse the order of their two names to conform with Western practice, which can confuse Americans who know that family names in China are traditionally placed first. For example, an American receiving a letter from Minwen Zhang, M.D., might mistakenly begin his reply, "Dear Dr. Minwen."

There is no foolproof way to avoid this kind of mistake, but there is one useful rule of thumb. More than 95 percent of Chinese family names are one-syllable words, including the ten or twelve most common ones. But Chinese given names are often two syllables. In the case of the two names Zhang and Minwen, one could be virtually certain that Zhang is the family name and Minwen is the given name.

Alas, not all Chinese given names are two syllables. More and more young people in China, especially in Beijing and the northern provinces, have one-syllable names. In the case of names such as Chen Qin and Zhao Zhe, for example, the American who does not recognize the one hundred or so most common Chinese family names is reduced to guessing or asking. (In these examples, Chen and Zhao are the family names.)

An Overview of Chinese Forms of Address

The Chinese have a much wider range of official titles and formal address forms than Americans, with many Chinese terms having no counterpart in English. The Chinese routinely use many more occupation-linked titles (such as doctor, professor, and major) than do Americans.

Even within Chinese families, older members are virtually always referred to and addressed by younger members according to their formal roles within the family—older brother, cousin, sister-in-law, and so forth—rather than by their given names. But older members typically use given names when addressing their juniors.

A valid generalization about the Chinese, then, is that they prefer formality when addressing one another in the course of daily life. In the limited number of situations where they feel that an informal address is appropriate, they have two alternatives. The first is to use the person's given name, a practice limited to close relatives and friends. The more common alternative is to add an age-relative prefix—*xiao* for those younger than oneself, *lao* for those older than oneself—to the family name of the person being addressed. (More information about xiao and lao appears later in this chapter.)

In China, forms of address have been affected by the political climate in a way that has no parallel in the United States. In the 1950s, shortly after the People's Republic of China was founded, the equalizing term *tongzhi* (comrade) was widely used because words denoting hierarchical rank were politically improper. In the late 1960s and early 1970s during the Cultural Revolution, teams of workers assumed power in most institutions. They tended to address one another using the term *shifu* (master worker), a form that became so widespread it was applied even to those who were anything but master workers. In the 1980s, when China was intent on opening itself to the outside world, forms of address paralleling Mr., Mrs., Miss, and Ms. in the West were revitalized. Today, Chinese who work in foreign-owned companies and joint-venture enterprises often take on Western given names like David, Henry, Catherine, or Anne and are generally addressed as such.

Chinese Forms of Address Americans Should Use

The Chinese Equivalents of Mrs., Miss, Ms., and Mr.

Just as a Chinese person's given name normally follows his or her family name, so does a Chinese person's title. The Chinese man who in English would be called Mr. Li is Li *xiansheng* (literally, Li Mr.) in Chinese. Miss Chen in English is Chen *xiaojie* (literally, Chen Miss) in Chinese.

A woman in the PRC does not take her husband's family name but keeps that of her father. The Chinese word for a married woman, *nüshi*, is best translated as "Ms." ("miz"). Nüshi is actually a rather formal title for an adult woman having nothing to do with marriage. It is not unlike Madam in English. The Chinese in the PRC seldom use nüshi among themselves but welcome its use by foreigners. Indeed, you should use nüshi because the alternative commonly found in Chinese phrase books for tourists, *taitai*, means "Mrs." and therefore is not properly applied to a woman whose family name is that of her father.[1]

You may address any young woman who is not likely to be married as xiaojie; Miss Zhao would be Zhao xiaojie. This form of address is socially delicate in the case of women in their late twenties and early thirties, however, because it is widely assumed in China that by that age a woman should be married. If you do not know whether a woman of this age is married, address her as nüshi.

Suppose you were acquainted with a woman named Yang Yonglan who marries a man named Gao Longsheng. Prior to their marriage, you would have addressed her as Yang xiaojie (Miss Yang). After their marriage, you would address her as Yang nüshi. There would be no change in your address of Gao Longsheng as a result of his marriage; he would remain Gao xiansheng (Mr. Gao).

Chinese Official and Occupation-Linked Titles

Instead of using the Chinese equivalents of Mr., Miss, and Ms. or Mrs., the Chinese themselves usually use official and occupation-linked titles, especially for official correspondence and during formal occasions such as banquets. You should do likewise if you know the title.

Some Chinese titles are the equivalents of those in daily use in the United States: doctor, ambassador, mayor, lieutenant, detective, and so forth. Virtually all official and occupation-linked titles used in the United States have equivalents in the People's Republic; the only difference is that they are used more frequently in the PRC.

Many terms that Americans consider appropriate only for descriptive purposes are used in China as titles that recognize a person's rank and/or special skills. These are routinely appended to one's family name when he or she is addressed. For example, Lin Rongcheng is a minister in the cabinet; he is addressed by just about everyone as Lin *buzhang*, Minister Lin. Other terms in widespread and frequent use include the Chinese equivalents of manager, deputy manager, chief engineer, engineer, foreman, bureau director, workshop director, section head, accountant, (police) captain, editor-in-chief, hospital administrator, and literally dozens of others. There is some variation from institution to institution on the extent to which these occupation-linked terms are used, but generally it is safe to say that the use of such titles is stronger in inland provinces and rural areas than in coastal provinces and cities. (See Appendix B for a list of the most commonly used titles.)

At Chinese universities, titles such as president, chancellor, vice president, chairman, and so forth are used more frequently than they are in the United States. It is noteworthy, however, that the Chinese equivalents of professor and associate professor are used more frequently in correspondence than in face-to-face exchanges. Similarly, Chinese academics with doctorates are addressed by title in correspondence (and are usually represented as such on their calling cards) but are rarely verbally addressed as Doctor. Americans who have doctorates may find, however, that their Chinese students address them as Doctor both in and out of class.

A common word that does not have an exact equivalent in English is *laoshi*, which is used in educational institutions at all levels to designate anyone who teaches. For example, the primary-school teacher Zhao Shumei is Zhao laoshi; the university professor Dai Wangdao is Dai laoshi. *Laoshi* is usually translated as "teacher," but that is not really accurate. *Teacher* in English is used almost exclusively to designate, but not to address, people who are instructors below the university and college levels. Although *laoshi* does not indicate rank, it is a term of considerable respect. In fact, *laoshi* conveys more respect than *professor* does in English. The implication of addressing an instructor as laoshi is somewhat similar (in English) to followers addressing a religious sage as teacher. Chinese students are likely to address their Western instructors as Teacher Smith or Teacher Leonard, or simply Teacher.

The Informal Prefixes Xiao and Lao

The closest the Chinese come to being informal or familiar with people who are not their family members or most intimate friends is to use either *xiao* or *lao* followed by the person's family name. This is the only exception to the rule that the family name precedes the title. The student Li Changrong is called in this context Xiao Li, not Li xiao. Note also that xiao or lao may be used with persons of either sex (although lao tends to be used more frequently with males).

Xiao may be translated as "young" or "junior,"[2] *lao* as "old" or "senior." Which term is used depends on the relation between the ages of the speaker and the person spoken to. Though young children rarely use these words with other children, the general rule is this: an older person of any age calls a younger person with whom he or she is familiar Xiao So-and-so; a younger person calls an older person Lao So-and-so. People in their early thirties or even late twenties may be addressed using lao by younger people and those in their forties or fifties may be addressed using xiao by older longtime friends.

On rare occasions, when the speaker wishes to acknowledge the advanced age and exceptional venerability of the person addressed, lao is used following the family name. It is likely that you will never have an opportunity to use *lao* in this way.[3]

If you remain in frequent contact with the same Chinese for more than a few weeks, you are likely to begin using xiao and lao in your exchanges with them. The age-relative rule stated above will apply in many cases, but there are enough exceptions so that it would be wise to find out how each individual is usually addressed by Chinese friends and colleagues. If almost all Chinese call your interpreter Xiao Zhang, for instance, you should not call her Lao Zhang regardless of your relative ages.

Other Forms of Address Used in the PRC

A considerable number of Chinese address others with whom they are not well acquainted as tongzhi, although this form is not used as extensively as it was a decade ago. Though *tongzhi* is translated as "comrade," it usually does not indicate an affiliation with the Communist party. It is a general term used irrespective of age, rank, sex, or occasion. When hailing someone on the street to ask directions, a Chinese might call out, "Tongzhi!" We suggest you avoid this word, however, since some Chinese believe it should be used only among themselves.

Shifu was very popular during the Cultural Revolution. These days its use tends to be restricted to people in skill- and service-linked occupations, such as hotel staff members, plumbers, electricians, shop attendants, waiters, repair personnel, and, on some occasions, peddlers. Use shifu when addressing people in these occupational roles. But if you are dealing with a young female shop attendant or waitress, use xiaojie instead.

The Chinese often extend kinship terms to people not related by blood or marriage. The Chinese equivalents of grandpa, grandma, uncle, aunt, brother, and sister are even used by the Chinese when asking someone for directions in the street. One might say to an elderly gentleman, for example, "Grandpa, how do I get to the railway station?" A child might address an unknown adult as "aunt" or "uncle." But you should not use such kinship terms. (Additional advice about obtaining information from strangers is provided on pages 139–42.)

As noted earlier, the use of given names in China is limited, so your Chinese colleagues are likely to be reluctant to address you by your given name, even though you ask them to do so. If this happens, let the matter drop and try to be content with their more formal terms of address.[4]

In general, you should not address a Chinese person by his or her given name alone. The safest rule is to use the family name with a title (Mr. Zheng or Zheng xiansheng). A variation of this rule is that in some localities it is acceptable to use the family *and* given names (Zheng Biao) if your Chinese colleagues are doing so. There are two exceptions to this rule. If you receive an explicit invitation to address someone by his or her given name alone, do so. And if a Chinese person routinely uses initials in place of a given name (C. S. Ling) or has taken a Western given name (Catherine Ling), then you can probably take this as a blanket invitation to Westerners to address him or her using the given name only.

Informality and warmth are not synonymous. It is entirely possible to have close and caring relationships with people whom you do not call by their given names. These two factors—warmth of personal relations and informality of address—vary independently of one another in both China and the United States. The difference is that among the Chinese, people are highly unlikely to signal that they are feeling increasingly warm toward you by switching (or asking to switch) to your given name. In China, formality of address does not imply interpersonal coolness.

---

[1] Women in the People's Republic who were married before 1950 bear the family name of their husbands and should be addressed using *taitai*, as in Chen taitai (Mrs. Chen). Many ethnic Chinese women from Hong Kong, Taiwan, and elsewhere take the name of their husbands, even today, and therefore are properly addressed as *taitai*.

[2] *Xiao* doubles as the Chinese word for "little," but when used as a title it does not in any way belittle the person so addressed. *Xiao* is a diminutive; it is also quite positive.

[3] An American of our acquaintance tells us that he once seriously embarrassed himself by using *lao* inappropriately. He overheard a famous eighty-year-old scientist addressed as "Zhang lao." A few minutes later, the American addressed one of his Chinese colleagues, whose age was perhaps sixty years, as "Li lao." This appellation was met by loud, but also hurt, guffaws from Mr. Li as well as others within earshot. Even at age sixty, Mr. Li was not nearly venerable enough to be addressed with *lao* following his family name, for this form of address is reserved for a very small, highly prestigious group of older people within a community.

[4] If your family name is difficult for the Chinese to pronounce whereas your given name is relatively easy, you may find that some Chinese whom you see frequently will soon begin to address you by your title and given name, as in "Dr. Paul." In some cases, however, a Chinese person's calling you by your title and given name ("Mr. Bob" or "Mrs. Judy") may reflect a misunderstanding about the name order (given/family) commonly used in English.

3

Greetings, Conversations, and Farewells

Greetings among the Chinese

The most common form of greeting among the Chinese is *Ni hao*, usually translated as "Good day" or "Greetings" but literally meaning "You are well." The same greeting phrased as a question—"How do you do?" or "Are you well?"—is *Ni hao ma?* This is regarded as a friendly inquiry and thus is favorably accepted. Even if you learn nothing else in Chinese, it is always a plus for you to greet Chinese people using these phrases. You may use either on virtually any occasion regardless of the time of day or the social status of the person you are greeting. The response to your "Ni hao" is usually a return "Ni hao" from the other person.

For a very high-status person or someone whom you especially want to compliment, you might say *Nin hao* or *Nin hao ma?*; *nin* is a more polite form of "you," similar to the French *vous*, the Spanish *usted*, and the German *Sie*.

The Chinese have other ways of greeting each other that are different from typical English-language greetings. Acquaint yourself with these greeting rituals, because English-speaking Chinese frequently use them in English translation to greet their foreign friends and colleagues.

23

The most conventional way to greet a Chinese is simply to say his or her name, perhaps adding a term of respect. For instance, a person may say "Li xiansheng," meaning "Mr. Li," when he encounters Mr. Li on the street. A girl just back from school may call out "*Baba!*" (Daddy!) when greeting her father.

This type of greeting is extremely simple but may give an American the impression that the Chinese person is preparing to ask a question or make a comment. (Upon hearing "Professor Walton," the American's response is likely to be "Yes?") But no question or comment is forthcoming, because only a greeting is intended. A nonverbal clue to this fact is that one's name is spoken with a falling intonation, not a rising one, and is often accompanied with a slight nod or bow.

The person greeted should acknowledge the other person's presence. One may respond by also saying the other person's name. Another possibility is to inquire about the other person's well-being, much as is done in the United States. A third possibility is to make an appropriate statement of fact about the other person. (The father of the girl in the above example could say something such as "Oh, you're back.")

There are no direct equivalents in traditional Chinese to "Good morning," "Good afternoon," "Good evening," or "Good night." Newscasters now use *Zaoshang hao* and *Wanshang hao* when greeting the audience, but these are simply translations, respectively, of the English "Good morning" and "Good evening." One rarely hears people use these terms in ordinary exchanges. *Ni zao,* a near equivalent of "Good morning," is sometimes used, but it literally means "You are early." If in the morning you are greeted with *Ni zao* or simply *Zao,* you may respond by saying "Zao," "Ni zao," or "Ni hao."

A typical Chinese greeting is *Nar qu ya?* or sometimes *Ni qu nar?* both of which mean "Where are you going?" Although its typical use occurs when passing another person on the street or in a building, it is not a genuine question, because exact information is not being requested. (This convention is similar to the one governing "How are you?" in the United States, which is rarely answered with precise information about one's well-being.) You are likely to assume, however, that you are being asked about your next destination and may wonder why the Chinese is being inquisitive about your private life.

When greeted by an acquaintance who asks where you are going, respond either by naming your destination or by saying vaguely, "I'm going there" while gesturing with your head or hand slightly in the direction in which you are moving. You need give no precise information about your destination.

Another common form of greeting in Chinese is *Chi le ma?* which means "Have you eaten?" This greeting normally occurs around mealtimes but, like questions about your destination, is not a genuine request for information. Even more important, it is not an invitation to join the other person for the forthcoming meal. To the ears of Americans and other native English speakers, however, it sounds like the opening phrase of an invitation. A British teacher of English in China, Helen Oatey, reports her first encounter with this greeting.

> When I first went to Hong Kong a number of years ago, I had no idea either about the Chinese language or the culture. Shortly after my arrival, I went to the bank on my way to school. I was extremely surprised when the bank clerk asked me if I had had my lunch. In British culture, his question would be regarded as an indirect invitation to lunch, and between unmarried young people it indicates the young man's interest in dating the girl. Since he was a complete stranger, I was quite taken aback.[1]

The way to cope with this greeting is to say either "I've eaten" or "I'm going to eat soon," depending on your situation. You can be truthful about saying you are going to eat soon because this information is not likely to elicit an invitation from the other person. However, an exception may

26

occur if you have been greeted by a Chinese person who has extensive experience in English-speaking cultures. In this case, his or her greeting may be the beginning of an invitation to a meal, and you shouldn't miss it.

In most circumstances you should avoid responding to "Have you eaten?" by saying, "No, I haven't eaten," for if you say this, the other person may feel obligated to invite you for a meal. If he or she is unable to treat you to a meal, embarrassment may result.

One form of typical Chinese greeting that may be difficult to recognize as such is a casual statement of fact about what the other person is doing. Suppose you are writing a letter and a Chinese friend comes in. He may say something such as "Oh, you're writing a letter." Or he may ask, "Are you writing a letter home?" Among the Chinese, this type of comment is just another friendly greeting.

Actually, the Chinese often make casual comments about whatever another person is doing to show acknowledgment or solidarity. Suppose you are working at a computer and an arriving Chinese acquaintance remarks, "Oh, you're working at the computer." You may think that the Chinese is saying something patently obvious, but you must put aside this interpretation and regard such comments as functional greetings.

Respond to such greetings in vague terms. To the Chinese friend who enters while you are writing a letter, you could say, "No, I'm ordering some books." To the friend who comments that you are working at your computer, you may say, "Yes, I've been working for two hours now." To a colleague near the post office who notes that you appear to be on your way to mail a package, you might comment on her apparent activity by replying, "Yes. And you are on your way to teach your class." Keep in mind that the Chinese tendency is simply to take note of your apparent circumstances by way of friendly greeting.[2]

To an American, most Chinese greetings seem much too personal for the level of attachment existing between him or her and the Chinese acquaintance. The American's reaction is an indicator of one of the fundamental differences between Chinese and American cultures, for these highly personal greetings spring from the fact that the Chinese live in closer community than Americans do. In a Chinese community one tends to treat others as though they were members of one's own family, and they are greeted in much the same way as one would greet kinfolk. Many ritual greetings in the United States are more neutral, such as "Good afternoon," "Hello," and "What's happening?" But such greetings are usually too impersonal for the mutually dependent Chinese.

Although not part of traditional Chinese culture and still not practiced in remote rural areas, shaking hands has become quite common in the People's Republic. The Chinese tend to shake hands somewhat more frequently than Americans do—upon parting, to express gratitude, and upon greeting even after only a few days of absence from one another. Much as in the United States, both hands may be used to convey special warmth or feeling. In China, both men and women are obliged to stand when shaking hands.

We strongly recommend that your greetings of the Chinese not include kissing, hugging, or other physical contact beyond handshaking. Unless you are dealing with Chinese who have spent considerable time in the United States or other parts of the West where such greeting behavior is practiced, these nonverbal forms will not be appreciated and, indeed, may be misinterpreted.

Conversational Openers

Opening conversational topics in the United States tend to be impersonal, which allows the participants freedom to withdraw from the contact at an early stage if they wish. Unless the conversants are intimately associated, it is rare for them to begin by talking about personal matters. The classic conversational opener in the United States, the state of the weather, is popular because it is completely impersonal, is known about by both parties, and can be dealt with briefly in most cases (thus ending the interaction or leading to some other topic).

The Chinese may begin a conversation by discussing the weather only if it is really atrocious. But if the weather is good, it is rather rare to hear one Chinese say to another something such as "Beautiful day, isn't it?" In China, one may begin a conversation by noting some item in the daily news, discussing a sporting or entertainment event, or commenting on an occurrence within view. However, these openers tend to occur less frequently than in the United States.

Opening conversational topics in China tend to be personal. Between strangers, a typical opening question might be "Where do you work?" or "What's your job?" If the participants are already acquainted, initial questions are likely to be about the other person's family life, especially about his or her children.

Even though the Chinese with whom you converse may be relative strangers, it is entirely proper for you to ask about their families. In fact, it is recommended. The Chinese feel warmer toward one another—and will toward you—when information about children and family life is exchanged. Although it is not taboo to ask about one's spouse, some Chinese may feel inhibited about going into detail about a husband or wife; therefore, avoid focusing your question on the spouse. We suggest this all-purpose opening question: "How many people are in your family?"

Another good conversation starter is to ask where the other person was born and then to talk about each other's hometown. You have many possibilities in this case, for you can follow up by asking about the town's location, its crops and industries, the dialect, the cuisine, regional customs, and so forth. Most Chinese love to talk about their hometown and will happily tell you everything they know about it.

If you are at a banquet or are having a meal with a Chinese

acquaintance, you could ask some questions about Chinese food. China has many distinct regions and minority peoples with their distinctive cuisines, so food provides an endless variety of conversational pathways. Most Chinese are pleased to share what they know about various cuisines. Other impersonal topics include scenic spots and historical sights, customs and habits of the Chinese, sports, music, and folk arts. These topics are safe in the sense that they are unlikely to lead to a subtle cross-cultural misunderstanding of some kind. Keep in mind that you will be a better questioner and listener in your conversations with Chinese whom you've just met if you have done some reading about China.

Conversational Restrictions

In the United States, you do not ask anyone with whom you are not on extremely close terms about his or her sex life or income. You hesitate before asking people for detailed information about the state of their health or, especially with women, about their age. Americans also tend to stay away from politics and religion, especially in informal social conversation. Some of these same topics are avoided by the Chinese, but they also have other restrictions.

The taboo on talking about sex is stronger in China than in the United States. The great majority of Chinese feel inhibited regarding discussions of sexual matters. If you thoughtlessly bring up some topic touching on sex, you may find your interlocutor giggling in an almost uncontrollable way; laughing is one way the Chinese show nervousness and social discomfort. Back off. If you try to talk about sexual matters, you will very likely be viewed in an unfavorable light for a long time thereafter.

Discussions about income are not taboo among some Chinese, but increasingly people tend to avoid such discussions. Income-related topics are not welcome, especially among businesspeople. If you are asked what you earn at your job in the United States, give a vague answer or avoid answering as best you can.

Our advice is that you not ask the Chinese about their income, their budget or money-spending habits, or the money they have saved in the bank. The pay of virtually all Chinese is unbelievably low by U.S. standards (and low as well in comparison to what you will be earning if you are working in China). You are likely to be so astonished the first two or three times you ask about income that you may say something inappropriate. Even without your asking, however, one or two of your Chinese friends may voluntarily tell you the level of their income; when this happens, try not to appear incredulous and do not make any invidious comparisons between China and the United States.

Age is generally not a sensitive topic among the Chinese. You are likely to be asked your age, even by virtual strangers, and, with one exception, you are not likely to offend a Chinese person by asking about his or her age. The exception is middle-aged Chinese women, who rather recently have started to feel sensitive about the topic of their age.

Do not ask a Chinese woman who appears to be in her late twenties or early thirties whether she is married or has children. If she is married, she will volunteer that information soon enough. If she is not married, she will probably say nothing because unmarried women of her age are traditionally believed to be in a regrettable state of affairs. You will not want to embarrass her by calling attention to the fact that she is single.

The Chinese will want to know about your family. If you are over thirty, they may become embarrassed if you report that you have no children and especially if you confess that you are not married. (You may be told that you are "too particular.") Use the opportunity to explain that in the United States, marriage and childbearing tend to occur relatively late and that most Americans consider remaining single and childless an acceptable option in life.

Bertrand Russell once made the remark that the Chinese are among the most unreligious people on earth, and he was correct. Only a small minority are devout Buddhists and fewer still are Christians. Americans who introduce religion into conversations often find the Chinese genuinely perplexed despite long, thoughtful explanations. But if you are asked direct questions touching on religion, by all means answer them to the best of your ability.

Although it is possible to talk about world news with any of your Chinese acquaintances in a general way, it may not be advisable to introduce discussions of a deeply political nature. Most Chinese are ready to tell you about their experiences during the Cultural Revolution and to discuss the ramifications of that interlude in recent Chinese history, but when it comes to current Chinese politics, they may become reticent if you are not one of their trusted friends. Most important, avoid becoming involved in intense discussions about the top leaders of the People's Republic; never strongly criticize those leaders, even in a joking manner. If a Chinese acquaintance does so, let the matter drop.

Farewells among the Chinese

Ordinary, daily farewells among both Chinese and Americans can occur in two phases. In the first phase, the idea is explicitly introduced that one or more of the parties should depart. In the second phase, one or more of the parties actually does depart from the home, office, or other location.

Among Americans, phase one tends to be played out as follows. One of the individuals initiates this phase by noting that he or she should depart soon, but no immediate move to depart is actually made. Both continue their conversation or other shared activity for a while longer; this delay may last from a few minutes to as much as an hour. Sometimes additional comments or moves to depart (such as rising from a chair) are made by the person who intends to depart, but these do not necessarily lead to his or her immediate departure. An exception occurs when someone suddenly discovers that a vitally important event will be missed if he or she does not depart at once; in this case, abrupt moves to depart will occur but with apologies.

Typical of phase one among Americans is that the person who intends to depart explains that a factor in his or her own personal situation compels the departure. For example, someone may say, "I've got to study for that math test tomorrow, so I'd better be going." Sometimes Americans excuse themselves because of some factor in the other person's life—"I know you need to get back to work, so I'm going to go now"— but this type of justification is not often thought necessary in a culture where each individual is expected to look out for his or her own welfare.

Among the Chinese from the PRC, phase one tends to occur in a very short period of time. Not uncommonly, the time is so short that it appears abrupt to an American, perhaps to the point of seeming to be motivated by displeasure or intentional rudeness; however, phase one is almost always very short among the Chinese themselves. At that point in the conversation or other activity when one of the individuals thinks it is time to leave, he or she announces that fact and immediately prepares to leave. If two people are sitting and talking in an apartment, for instance, the one who is the guest may say something appropriate and simultaneously rise and walk directly to the door.

When the Chinese offer a reason for leaving, it is unlikely to be related to the leaver's own personal situation. The explanation more often will be related to the other person's presumed needs. For example, in a meeting between people in superior and subordinate roles, the subordinate is likely to relate his or her imminent departure to a disinclination to "take up any more of your time." (He or she might even offer an apology such as "I've wasted so much of your valuable time.") In the collectivist culture of China, a person is not expected to emphasize personal needs as a reason for acting.

When phase two arrives, the characteristics of American and Chinese cultures are reversed. After an American who is leaving actually goes to the door (thus ending phase one), his or her exit from the scene (phase two) occurs quite efficiently. The person remaining behind accompanies the leaver to the door and may even step outside to offer a farewell wave as the departing guest disappears.

Among the Chinese, phase two is typically played out over an extended time—and over an extended space. The two people exit from the door together and continue walking some distance while continuing to converse. The distance that the host accompanies a guest is an indication of the esteem in which he or she is held. It is not uncommon for a host to accompany the guest down several flights of stairs and out of the building before saying the final good-bye. If the host wishes to show especially high regard, he or she continues to converse with the guest while walking to the bicycle rack, the compound gate, or even the bus stop (where a good host continues to converse until the bus arrives). The host waves good-bye and calls out "*Zaijian*" (literally, "again to see") as the guest finally disappears.

Whenever Chinese guests come to visit you in your home or office, it is important that you accompany them beyond the door when they depart. If you neglect this ritual, those guests who are less familiar with American culture may feel that you have slighted them.

What about telephone farewells? Leave-taking via the telephone cannot be easily divided into two phases. We can say, though, that typical telephone farewells among the Chinese are similar to phase one of their typical face-to-face farewells: seemingly abrupt. You may be left holding a dead receiver in astonishment on many occasions before you become accustomed to the way in which Chinese acquaintances both announce the end of a phone conversation and simultaneously act upon it. Simply put, what you hear is "Good-bye," click.[3]

[1] Helen Oatey, "Chinese and Western Interpersonal Relationships," in *Intercultural Communication: What It Means to Chinese Learners of English*, edited by Hu Wenzhong (Shanghai: Shanghai Translation Publishing House, 1988), 48.

[2] An American acquaintance of ours tells this story. While working in China, he was greeted every day by his Chinese housekeeper upon his return from the office. She invariably said, "Oh, you've come back." After this occurred many times, he finally asked her about it. "So, are you asking me if I'm back, which you can plainly see, or are you telling me I'm back, which I can plainly see?" The woman laughed uproariously and a bit sheepishly, but she could not explain her manner of greeting—except to say that it was precisely what the situation called for, and called for every day.

[3] The abruptness of Chinese telephone farewells may be due to linguistic inadequacy as well as lack of knowledge about appropriate telephone etiquette when conversing in English via the telephone. When two Chinese are conversing via telephone, clues are given by the parties when they intend that the conversation should soon terminate, but (as is sometimes the case between Americans) the actual process of bringing the conversation to a close can be protracted.

4

四

Chinese-Style Dining

The Significance of Dining

People in China like to join their friends on informal walks or bicycle rides and institutionally organized picnics, and they occasionally treat themselves to a theatrical event (such as Peking opera) or, if they are entertaining guests, a sightseeing excursion (such as a visit to the Great Wall). Dining, however, is clearly their entertainment of choice. Even when they enjoy each other's company during special occasions such as Spring Festival (the type of gathering an American might be tempted to call a party), they always include a full meal.

The type of gathering so common among Americans, where people nibble finger food and sip drinks while standing and talking, is only now appearing in China; in mainland China there is as yet no apt translation for *party*. Furthermore, it is rare for the Chinese to get together in a bar or pub to chat informally while sipping alcoholic beverages. (In south China, however, the indigenous teahouse serves a similar social function.)

Luncheon and, especially, dinner banquets are social occasions that the Chinese take seriously. Nevertheless, they are rather relaxed during these times. Non-Chinese guests should not be preoccupied with worries about proper protocol.

The Chinese Way of Dining

The following description of the procedures observed during a Chinese meal may be most accurate for the Beijing area (with which we are most familiar) but should be useful wherever you dine in the Chinese style. Of course, no generalized description can fit every case exactly.

Upon arrival, the guests are served hot tea or, if the weather is warm, soft drinks or other beverages. Snacks such as peanuts or sweets may be available. Host(s) and guests engage in conversation while sitting in comfortable chairs away from the table. When the food has been placed on the table, the host invites the guests to be seated there. (A guest should not go to the table without being invited.) At formal dinners the host will direct individuals to specific seats unless place cards have been set on the table.

Before the main dishes are served, there are normally three or four appetizers such as cold meat, thousand-year-old eggs, stir-fried cucumber, and boiled or fried peanuts. Each of the main dishes contains a separate kind of food—some with meat or fish, some without. If you eat at someone's home, all dishes (usually six to eight) are served at the same time. If you eat at a restaurant, the hot main dishes are normally served one at a time. Better restaurants have separate rooms that may be rented for private dinner parties. Often, karaoke facilities are provided. Waitresses are in attendance and help to put the food on each guest's plate. Whether you dine at a restaurant or someone's home, beer or wine is commonly served, and a selection of soft drinks is also available. Liquor may be served for the purpose of toasting, but you may toast with anything, even a soft drink. Mineral water may be available as a substitute for plain water. (Cold water and ice are usually not served in China; providing them can be a major undertaking not only for hosts in homes but for restaurants that are unaccustomed to Western guests as well.)

After the company has eaten its fill, the dishes are cleared away and, usually, soup appears. Soup served at this time may take the place of dessert. If there is another dessert, it is likely to be canned or fresh fruit or ice cream. Tea may be served at the end of the meal. (Coffee or after-dinner drinks are not served in China and should not be requested.)

Toasts and speeches are a feature of banquets and other formal meals given by Chinese hosts. Shortly after people have begun eating, the host is likely to make a short speech welcoming the guests and proposing a toast in their honor. The cohost may do likewise. At this time, the guests need only accept these gestures graciously. Near the end of the meal, roughly about the time the soup course is served, the senior guest should reciprocate by giving his or her own little speech of gratitude for the hospitality and proposing an appropriate toast. One or two other guests may do likewise as well.

The meal ends when the host thanks the guests for coming or offers a final toast; the serving of wet towelettes is another sign that the meal has concluded. (Unlike American practice, it is the host who takes the initiative in bringing the event to a close, not the guests.) After rising from the table, everyone present departs at once—abruptly, in fact, by American standards. The entire affair lasts about two hours.

Traditionally, it is the host's duty to ensure that guests are served and that food is added to their plates during the meal. Guests within reach of the host will be served personally by him or her, and guests not seated near the host may have their plates replenished by the persons sitting to their left and right. (Serving spoons or serving chopsticks are often used for this purpose.) However, Chinese hosts are increasingly asking their guests to help themselves instead of putting food on their plates. Some hosts start the meal by serving a helping of one dish to the guests sitting beside them and then say, "Please help yourselves after this."

It is not uncommon for the host or a Chinese seatmate to put portions of all the dishes onto your plate without asking what you want. If some dish, such as sea slug, is served to you without your desiring it, you may simply leave it uneaten on your plate. The same may be done in the case of food that is served after you are full. You may say you don't want a certain food or that you don't want any more food at all, but a Chinese host is likely to understand such a request in Chinese terms—as a sign of modesty that should not be interpreted literally. A nonverbal indicator that you do not wish to eat more is to leave some rice in your bowl or on your plate.

The preparation of Chinese food generally involves cutting or chopping all ingredients into pieces that are bite-sized (if they were not so already). No knives are available at the table, and there is no need—at least in theory—to use fingers. Since fingers are not intended to touch the food, napkins are not considered necessary. (However, they often turn up in restaurants and homes where Western influence is increasing.) Chopsticks, which are used either to grasp the food, to lift it from underneath, or to push it from plate to mouth, are considered sufficient for all purposes except the eating of soup or ice cream, for which spoons are provided.

Two exceptions to this general rule are worth noting. One of the most delicious of all Chinese specialties, Peking duck, is eaten with the fingers. Eating Peking duck involves wrapping strips of meat and other items in a thin pancake, a process difficult to complete with chopsticks (though consummate chopstick masters can manage it). Since fingers can be used in this case, wet towels are brought to the table just before the duck is served so that guests may wash their hands. Napkins or additional wet towels are provided during the eating process. The second (and more common) exception occurs when fruit is served whole as a dessert; eating this also involves the fingers.

A few types of Chinese food elude the chopstick skills of

most Westerners. Chicken, for example, is often prepared by simply chopping the carcass, bones and all, into pieces about the size of golf balls. Since bones remain, eating the pieces with chopsticks is quite a challenge. Even some Chinese appear to have difficulty. Fish (including shellfish), often memorably delicious, may also involve difficult manipulations.

Anyone going to China should attempt to find someone who knows how to use chopsticks and who can provide a lesson or two. Nevertheless, Western cutlery is widely available in China, sometimes even in the homes of ordinary people; Westerners who have not mastered chopsticks should not be embarrassed to ask if a knife and fork are available.

In the United States, parts of food that cannot be eaten (such as bones) are usually placed to the side of one's plate. Food that accidentally falls onto the table may be retrieved and eaten. But among the Chinese, food that cannot be eaten is deposited on the table in the vicinity of one's plate. Food that accidentally falls onto the table is usually not retrieved and eaten.

Most Americans were brought up to believe that, while dining, a person (1) should not smack the lips, slurp liquids, or make any other loud noises with the mouth, (2) should never bring the edge of a plate or bowl into contact with the mouth, (3) should not smoke at the table except with permission of the others present, and (4) should not spit anything onto the table or floor. Chinese table etiquette is different. You can expect all of the above when dining informally with some Chinese. At formal dinners and banquets, however, the rules governing Chinese dining are basically the same as in the West.

During any Chinese meal, guests should make appreciative remarks about at least some of the dishes on the table and about the general quality of the event. Remarks of this kind should be repeated at the end of the affair, too, especially by those who have been sitting far away from the host(s) during the meal. It is not adequate to limit these compliments solely to the time of one's departure.[1]

For readers who may be attending or giving banquets in the People's Republic, additional advice and guidelines are available in part II.

---

[1] Beware of praising (for the sake of politeness) foods that you do not care for very much. You may be served them at subsequent banquets or dinner parties given by the same host.

5

五

Appointments, Visiting, and Time Use

Time-Use Patterns in Official Chinese Contexts

American diplomats, trade representatives, businesspeople, and others who are meeting with Chinese officials from government, industry, education, and the like can expect time-use patterns that are similar to internationally recognized practices. Meetings are by appointment only, the visitors are expected to arrive on time, the duration of the meetings (except for negotiating sessions) is rarely more than one hour, and certain signals, usually by the host, indicate that the meeting should end.

Appointments with Chinese officials can be made by letter or telephone. When meeting high-level officials, you should make your request at least two weeks in advance. For mid-level officials, appointments should be made not less than one week in advance. If you know someone who can act as a go-between to arrange your meeting with an official, ask him or her to perform this function for you. The nature of your business should be clearly stated at the time the appointment is made.

Since punctuality is important, allowances should be made for the possibility of transportation problems. If you arrive early, so much the better, as it is likely to be seen as a sign of respect for the official you are meeting. (This is not to say that the official will appear at once to receive you.) If you are unavoidably compelled to be late, offer a sincere apology as well as a brief explanation.

The time devoted to official meetings at higher levels tends to be tightly circumscribed. It is not unusual for such meetings to last only half an hour. Often, when the appointment is made, the length of the meeting will be specified. Some meetings during which extensive negotiations must take place run well over an hour, but these are exceptions to the rule. It is uncommon for meetings to be held in the same room where the official has his or her desk. Most meetings are held over tea in a large reception room with comfortable chairs.

Be alert for signals by a Chinese host that the meeting should end within the next few minutes. An offer to ask the attendants to bring more tea may be a subtle hint that the meeting should be ending; in this case, your proper response is to decline the offer and say that you should be leaving quite soon. Another signal is that the host will sum up what has been said. If the Chinese official thanks you for coming, the meeting is nearing its end. If all else fails, your host will stand up as a preface to leading you and other visitors out of the reception room.

Time-Use Patterns in Nonofficial Chinese Contexts

There are a number of differences between Chinese and Americans in their use of time in nonofficial contexts. One of your first big surprises is likely to occur when a Chinese visitor arrives early. Not two or three minutes early, but fifteen or more minutes. Since there is rarely a receptionist or secretary to deal with your guest, the situation can be quite awkward. What do you do, for example, when you've come out of the bath to shout "Who is it?" through the door and, being naked and wet, have no option but to leave your visitor shuffling around in the hallway?

If asked why they have arrived so early, the Chinese may reply that they do not wish to waste the host's valuable time. (The apparent logic of this response is that if the meeting can be completed before the time it was scheduled to begin, then none of the host's time has been wasted.) Our view, however, is that their motive for arriving early is to demonstrate deep respect for the host, who at this point is invariably someone with whom they are not well acquainted. As the relationship grows warmer over subsequent days and weeks, the Chinese arrive less and less early until, finally, they settle into their standard pattern: arriving more or less on time.

The nature of traditional visiting practices may help to explain why the Chinese are less aware than Americans of the difficulties potentially caused by very early arrivals. Among peasants and other Chinese connected with agriculture, no prior arrangement is thought necessary for any kind of gathering of friends or family members. In the countryside, one may arrive at a friend's home without prior notice and may enter without waiting to be admitted. Regardless of whether one wishes to see a friend to discuss a specific issue or merely to pass the time of day, one simply walks in, perhaps calling out the name of the person being sought. Homes are open to their owners' friends all the time. The concept of privacy as we understand it in individualistic Western cultures does not exist in the traditional collectivist culture of China. (When *privacy* is translated into Chinese, the term *yinsi* is often employed; it means "hidden private affairs" and thus carries the connotation of shady dealing and deceptive secrecy.)

With the dramatic increase of home phones and even cellular phones in the cities, unannounced visiting has become less common. Educators, scientists, technicians, and people in similar professions schedule their time carefully; to Chinese as well as Western businesspeople and managers, "time is money." Although dropping into someone's office just to say hello is still possible, the general rule is that if you wish to see someone on business, prior arrangement is necessary. (Even before neighbors in large cities visit each other, they usually phone first to make sure that they will be welcome.)

Regardless of these gradual changes, the norm still prevails that one may visit a very close friend at his or her office without prior notice at almost any time. One need wait outside only if other people whom one does not know are already inside.

Some Chinese families in urban areas are developing guidelines regarding the times when they prefer to receive visitors in their homes. For example, some families may say that you are welcome to visit during Saturday afternoon or at any time on Sunday. These are genuine open hours; still, there are restrictions to keep in mind. Unless you are on exceptionally friendly terms, you should not arrive during early afternoon or at suppertime. In the People's Republic, noon to 1:00 P.M. is the time for lunch and 1:00 to 2:30 is the time for *wushui*, the afternoon nap.[1] Supper is usually eaten between 6:00 and 7:00. (These times might be slightly earlier during the winter and slightly later during the summer.) You should never arrive earlier than 9:00 A.M. or later than 8:00 P.M.

Because of your cultural conditioning, it may be difficult for you to fully adopt the traditional Chinese habit of showing up for a visit without any prior knowledge of the host's preferences regarding impromptu visits. But if you do come to feel comfortable enough to attempt unannounced visiting of Chinese friends, keep the following in mind: if you unexpectedly come into a household during a meal, you will probably be invited to join the family at table. This invitation, though polite, is probably not genuine, so you should decline it and depart unless a truly energetic and convincing effort is made to persuade you to remain. If you unexpectedly come into a household shortly before a meal, you may take the host's invitation to join the family at table as the signal to excuse yourself and depart. But you should be prepared to change your mind in the face of earnest and repeated entreaties to remain.

For Americans, visiting Chinese friends is not likely to require major adjustments. Since you are culturally conditioned to make appointments for all types of visits and to be punctual, you are not likely to cause annoyance or misunderstanding by showing up at the wrong time. If there is any danger, it is that you will unnecessarily isolate yourself from your Chinese friends by feeling reluctant to visit them without having a definite invitation.

Receiving Social Visits from Chinese Friends

A major adjustment some Americans must make involves visits from their Chinese acquaintances and friends and, in some cases, from their Chinese business counterparts as well. As we have seen, the Chinese are prone to visit others without prior notice and occasionally at a time of day when no American would even dream of turning up. Foreign teachers in the People's Republic are especially likely to receive such visits from their students. Unannounced visiting at odd hours is a practice that seems intended to exasperate Americans, whose native culture encourages them to believe their home is their castle. As though all this were not enough, Chinese visitors sometimes remain far too long by American standards.

In a culture of individualism such as that of the United States, the concept of privacy extends not only to one's personal space and possessions but also to one's time. Individualists are not hermits, of course. They expect to share their possessions, their living space, and their time with others. But they also expect to have some control over these matters, even when family members and good friends are the "others" in question. They want others to recognize their right to dictate the rules under which their space, possessions, and time are shared. With respect to time, individualists assume that it is reasonable, even necessary, for a person to be alone during certain portions of each day.

In the traditional agrarian culture of China, people recognize that certain spaces and objects are identified with a particular person or family. (The concept of theft is certainly recognized in China.) Largely absent from traditional Chinese culture, however, is the notion that the person can therefore expect family members and good friends to refrain from entering those spaces without his or her implicit, if not explicit, permission. Furthermore, your time is not assumed to be under your exclusive control, to be shared with others or reserved for self as you see fit. In traditional Chinese culture, the basic social unit is the group, not the individual. So if a friend or relative apparently prefers to spend significant portions of time in solitary pursuits, this is viewed as perplexing if not actually an indication of selfishness.[2]

Many Americans who interact frequently with the Chinese spend most of their time with businesspeople and professionals who are moving away from the traditional time-use patterns of the countryside. But some Americans (such as teachers in China located away from large urban areas) do not. When these Americans become friendly with local people who have been little influenced by Western values regarding time and space, conflicts may occur. Chinese people from a rural background are not apt to share American assumptions about making appointments or about appropriate times for visiting.

If you teach at a Chinese university, it is possible that some of your students may visit you without prior notice and sometimes at odd hours. Some Americans have learned to cope with these difficulties effectively; we can pass their strategies along to you. The key is that you must take what might be called "the cultural line," explaining whenever appropriate that, as a typical American, you enjoy having visitors but do have certain customs that you've become used to and prefer to have observed by all potential guests. Continue by stating certain visiting guidelines, such as (1) the days of the week when you will be happy to receive guests, (2) the times during those days when you will be prepared to receive guests, and (3) the time of evening when you will expect guests to depart. An alternative is to state those times of the day and week when you do not wish to have guests. We suggest that you formulate a set of guidelines at the very beginning of any potentially extensive contacts you expect to have with the Chinese. State these guidelines to groups and individuals whenever possible.

Some Americans report exasperation because their Chinese guests stay far too long. We view this difficulty as rooted in subtle cultural differences. In the United States, the rule covering almost all types of social occasions is that it is the guest's responsibility to determine the time of his or her departure. In China, with respect to relatively formal occasions, guests await the host's signal for them to leave because doing otherwise tends to undermine the dignity of the affair as well as the harmony of their relationship with the host. This rule does not necessarily carry over to informal occasions, but it does establish a precedent that makes it reasonable for you to signal when it's time for your guests to depart, even when the gathering is anything but formal.

Learn to use the signals employed by Chinese hosts. Start by using the same hints that would apply in the United States: glancing at your watch, stifling yawns, offering to make another pot of tea, or standing up. If your indirect or nonverbal hints are ineffective, you will have to use more direct strategies. If the context allows, you can thank your guests for coming to see you and say something appropriate about seeing them again in the future. Another recourse is for you to state, politely and with an ostensible rationale ("I must arise early tomorrow in order to..."), that you wish to retire for the night and will therefore say good-bye. If you have previously announced a preferred departure time, it may be sufficient for you to note that the time has arrived and to inform the company that they will be welcome at some future time. Be sure that you accompany your guests at least to the outside door of your building, perhaps farther; doing so indicates the esteem in which you hold them.

Some Americans may face the problem of being isolated due to the absence of visits by Chinese colleagues and acquaintances. The possibility does exist that having no visitors carries some kind of negative message, such as disapproval of your behavior or embarrassment over your loss of face. Much more likely, however, your Chinese colleagues and acquaintances are simply too shy or otherwise inhibited to take the initiative. Fortunately, you are culturally conditioned as an American to take the initiative yourself, so if you feel isolated, you should not hesitate to invite your Chinese acquaintances to be your guests or to join you in some activity. (Informal, low-cost social occasions are preferred by most Chinese.) They will appreciate your invitation and may be less inhibited about making spontaneous visits to you after you have broken the ice.

A Word about Hosting Chinese Visitors in the United States

In China, guests are usually treated as though they were members of the host's primary group. A Chinese host's responsibility, therefore, is more extensive than that of an American host, for he or she must not only fulfill needs and provide amenities but also offer continuous solicitous care and protection to the guests. These expectations should be kept in mind by Americans who are hosting Chinese visitors. American hosts typically assume that guests wish to have unstructured time to be alone or pursue their own interests, which is a valid assumption in a culture that stresses individualism and self-reliance. But Chinese visitors who have no previous experience with Western values and practices may become unhappy if deprived of more or less constant attention by their hosts.

If you are preparing to host Chinese visitors, perhaps the best advice is this: give them more attention than you ordinarily would visiting Americans or Western Europeans, but not so much that you yourself become overburdened and annoyed by the process.[3]

---

[1] *Wushui*, the nap taken just after lunch, is a tradition that is gradually declining in Beijing and other major urban areas. But it continues to be quite prevalent among the Chinese elsewhere, so you must take it into account when planning your visits. Summer wushui may last from 1:00 to 2:30 (the hottest part of the day), whereas winter wushui is more likely to last from 1:00 to 2:00.

[2] An American acquaintance of ours reports that Sundays were her time for reading and other solitary pursuits while she was working as a lawyer in Beijing. Her Chinese driver, however, repeatedly offered to take her to parks and other public places on Sundays. He would try to persuade her to come by saying, "It's not good for you to be alone!"

[3] For more information on hosting Chinese in the United States, consult the following.

Scott D. Seligman. *Dealing with the Chinese: A Practical Guide to Business Etiquette in the People's Republic Today.* New York: Warner Books, 1989. See chapter 11, "Hosting the Chinese." Revision forthcoming, 1999.

6

六

Chinese Modesty and Humility

Chinese Disparagement of Themselves and Their Families

One of the surprises many Americans experience when interacting with the Chinese occurs when they give a sincere compliment to a Chinese acquaintance only to hear denial in return. For instance, an American might say to her interpreter, "Your English is really very good." A typical reply would be, "Oh, no! My English is very poor." In Chinese the response would likely include the phrase *Bu hao, bu hao!* meaning "Not good, not good!" Another common denial is *Nali, nali?* which literally means "Where, where?" To most Americans, such responses are likely to seem ungrateful or even a bit impolite.

The Chinese are unlikely to respond to a compliment with thanks or any other acknowledgment of its validity. To do so would demonstrate a lack of the indispensable virtue of humility. Chinese people's concern for humility is apparent everywhere. For example, Americans who are invited to a Chinese home for dinner often find the table overflowing with six to eight beautifully presented, mouthwatering dishes.

The host or hostess is likely to comment (in a suitably apologetic tone of voice), "We hope you won't mind joining our simple home meal. We're not very good at cooking, so we've only prepared a few dishes for this evening." Or an American who reads Chinese may discover upon admiring the exquisite paintings of a renowned artist that he or she has written characters in the corner that mean "trying one's hand" or "daubing."

In his essay "The Importance of Being KEQI," Yao Wei offers an example of Chinese humility. The Chinese word *keqi* in Yao's title is usually translated as "courteous" or "polite," but it connotes more. Courtesy in China often requires a ritual in which self-deprecation plays a central role. Such a ritual is the focus of Yao's story, in which a Chinese carpenter who has emigrated to the United States goes to a furniture company looking for a job. He is a highly skilled maker of tables with twenty-five years of experience. Yao portrays the interview dialogue as follows.

Employer: Have you done carpentry work before?

Carpenter: I don't dare say that I have. I have just been in a very modest way involved in the carpenter trade.

Employer: What are you skilled in then?

Carpenter: I won't say "skilled." I have only a little experience in making tables.

Employer: Can you make something now and show us how good you are?

Carpenter: How dare I be so indiscreet as to demonstrate my crude skills in front of a master of the trade like you.[1]

As Yao points out, an American employer at this point might very well show the humble Chinese applicant to the door. But, were he to persist in requesting a sample, the Chinese carpenter would finally (and with continuing expressions of humility as he worked) fashion a veritable work of art, which, no doubt, he would describe as the work of a beginner even as the employer admired his speed and skill.

Well-mannered Chinese deprecate not only their own accomplishments and advantages but also those of their family members. In a highly family-oriented society, praising family members is tantamount to praising oneself. And saying thank you to a compliment regarding a family member is the same as accepting without protest a compliment about oneself, a sure sign of bad manners.

The Chinese habit of disparaging themselves, their creations, and their family members may lead you to conclude that you should offer no compliments to your Chinese acquaintances. But that is the wrong conclusion. The Chinese like to receive compliments just as much as you do; they merely respond to them differently.

There is one exception. You must not openly admire the appearance of a member of the opposite sex with whom you are not on intimate terms. In the United States, this type of compliment is fairly common and can occur without implying that a romantic liaison is desired. Not so among the Chinese, where such a compliment could easily be interpreted as a sexual overture. The response would be not only one of denial but also acute embarrassment.

On the other hand, any tendency you may have to admire and praise young children will be greatly appreciated by the Chinese. Most dote on their children and can be seen beaming with pride when someone remarks on their fine behavior or appearance, though they will often offer the usual ritual denial.

Other Behavioral Features of Chinese Humility

When the Chinese meet for the first time in social situations, they tell each other their names and identify their work units, but they seldom mention their titles or otherwise identify their positions in the hierarchy of their work units. Likewise, in correspondence it is unusual for a Chinese to list his or her title or similar information below the signature, as is customary in the United States.

Business cards are increasingly used by the Chinese. They are exchanged at many social gatherings and clipped to correspondence when the recipient is someone with whom the writer is not acquainted. The use of a business card to inform others of one's title or position is considered more refined than stating this information verbally or adding it to the bottom of a letter. If you are going to have extensive business or professional contacts with the Chinese, carry business cards with English on one side and Chinese on the other. (This will require that you find a Chinese acquaintance who can give you a Chinese name.)

Chinese academics, professionals, and technicians increasingly prepare and distribute résumés, and you should do so too. (Rarely is it necessary to have it translated into Chinese.) Use your résumé when you are seeking a job with a Chinese organization where you are unknown, but do not distribute it to people who already know you; to do so is to demonstrate a lack of humility.

Being a good listener is considered good manners among the Chinese, but some people are obligated to listen more than others. Young Chinese show humility and good upbringing to their elders by listening much and speaking little. Subordinates show deference to their supervisors in the same way. Senior people in China generally have great freedom to talk because juniors demonstrate their place in the hierarchy by giving humble attention most of the time.

During conversations, the Chinese can maintain silence for a much longer time than Americans, who feel acutely uncomfortable when there are silent interludes in a conversation and will say something—anything—to end a silence after about twenty seconds. A parallel situation is rather unlikely among the Chinese because the junior people will have learned to wait for their seniors to continue speaking. Discomfort occurs if a junior person speaks out of turn, not if two or three speaking turns go unfilled by talk.

Humility vis-à-vis seniors applies not only to conversational practices but also to other types of social situations. An amusing example occurs when a large number of Chinese prepare themselves for a group photograph. All understand that the front row, especially the center-front location, is the place of honor and recognize that proper humility requires that they not willingly place themselves in the front. Even the senior people usually try to remain away from the front row, with the result that everyone begins to crowd into the back row(s). After some good-natured scuffling and earnest appeals from the junior members and the photographer to the senior ones, the situation resolves itself properly. If you are to be included in a group photograph, you should, of course, begin by heading toward the back row and should move forward, if at all, only after the Chinese make several sincere appeals for you to do so.

When a speaker or honored guest is introduced to a room full of people in the United States, he or she customarily is welcomed by a round of applause. The person so welcomed is expected to show his or her appreciation by smiling, perhaps waving, then waiting until the applause dies down. Speakers and guests are welcomed in the same way in China, but their response is different: they are expected to join in the applause. If you were to demonstrate the typical American response to applause, you might be viewed as conceited by many in the audience. Instead, you should "clap back." Clapping back is not regarded as lacking in humility but as a way of showing appreciation for the welcome as well as solidarity with those who are clapping.

The value placed by Americans on personal assertiveness is not well received by the Chinese. Western culture, and to some extent business culture everywhere, is grounded in competitive values, and these values are beginning to filter into the PRC. Selling oneself is necessary to some extent almost anywhere in the world in order to make a sale or land a desirable assignment. But how one competes and how one sells oneself differ from culture to culture. Traditional Chinese values require that a person who wishes to make a favorable impression avoid being self-congratulatory or personally assertive. Consequently, it is wise to be modest about your personal capabilities and experience. Boasting about the qualities of your company's product or service, however, is becoming increasingly acceptable. Unless direct, specific questions are asked by Chinese associates, you should not volunteer information beyond your name and your company or agency affiliation before discussing whatever business is at hand.

The Origin and Nature of Chinese Humility

Valuing humility is part of centuries-old Chinese tradition. We do not know when many of the behavioral practices associated with humility originated, but we do know that, linguistically, a series of honorific and self-deprecating terms was in use more than two thousand years ago. During the millennia that followed, many set phrases and words were used to demonstrate the absence of self-centeredness or personal assertiveness. For example, *biren*, which means "my humble self," was in common use for centuries and is heard occasionally even now. Many other expressions conveyed the same idea; most are nearly obsolete, but others can still be heard in remote areas of China. When these terms are translated into English, some sound so self-disparaging that they make Americans feel uncomfortable.

In contemporary times, other expressions have been developed to serve the same general purpose, and you may hear some of them in daily English or Chinese conversation. One is "My immature opinion is...," which is often a preamble for someone's proposal even though that proposal may be very well thought-out. Another, used to describe a dinner that may be truly sumptuous, is "an informal meal." And a well-furnished apartment with entirely adequate sanitary facilities is likely to be described as "an apartment with poor conditions." This type of expression is used not only in reference to one's own ideas and characteristics but also in describing one's possessions and creations.

To enhance harmony and avoid friction, the Chinese are taught at an early age to keep themselves in check, to be tolerant of others, and to defer to the desires of the family as determined by consensus or by the decision of the oldest male. One of the famous sayings of Confucius is "Let the emperor be an emperor, the subject a subject, the father a father, and the son a son," the implication being that within the family as within the nation, personal desires are best subjugated to the will of the patriarch. Another concern of Confucius was that each person in the hierarchy should be involved in activity appropriate to his or her rank and station. Being a subject or a son was not a matter of total passivity; being an emperor or a father was not a matter of freedom from all obligations. Chinese collectivism requires harmonious interaction from group members at all levels.

Whenever you deal with the Chinese, we suggest that you do everything possible to ensure that your own speech and writing convey a sense of humility. Of course, this will be difficult for people from the United States, a culture that stresses individualism heavily. But it will be worth the effort.

Incidentally, an increasing number of younger Chinese are adopting behavior patterns that seem to run counter to traditional principles of modesty. For example, it is quite common for entertainers to say thank you when they are praised face-to-face by the host or hostess of the evening.[2] Therefore, you should be prepared for situations in which your Chinese associates behave much the same as their counterparts in the West.

---

[1] Yao Wei, "The Importance of Being KEQI: A Note on Communication Difficulties," in *Communicating with China*, edited by Robert A. Kapp (Yarmouth, ME: Intercultural Press, 1983), 73.

[2] An investigation conducted by some M.A. students at Beijing Foreign Studies University a few years ago revealed that about 70 percent of the young people surveyed tended to accept compliments instead of trying to deny them. In 1995, a researcher did an investigation among second-year students in the English and Chinese Departments of Xinxiang Teachers College in Henan Province. This study revealed that English majors responded in the affirmative in 90 percent of the situations under investigation, while 88 percent of the Chinese majors responded in the affirmative. This seems to indicate that young people tend to accept compliments in most cases regardless of their specialization.

Making Friends with the Chinese

Levels of Personal Relationships among the Chinese

In the United States people maintain personal relationships at various levels of intimacy (including no intimacy at all) and for a variety of emotional and practical reasons. The same is true in China. According to Chinese social psychologist Hwang Kwang-kuo, relationships in Chinese society tend to fall into three categories.[1]

1. Affective ties: These deep, intimate relationships which bind family members and close friends together are the most important human ties among the Chinese. Resources are distributed among people with affective ties according to the "need rule": those who have resources distribute them freely to those in need. Ongoing mutual dependency characterizes such relationships, though who is dependent upon whom may change over the years (as in the case of parents and children). Affective ties are formed early in life and last a lifetime.

    Affective ties are unlikely to be formed by Americans or other foreigners with Chinese acquaintances (exceptions could occur, for example, in cases where an American marries into a Chinese family). We say little about affective ties in this chapter because unique factors such as an individual's parentage, birthplace, and personal traits are key factors in the development of such ties.

2. Instrumental ties: These relationships, which are usually temporary and often anonymous, enable the parties to attain practical ends. The "equity rule" characterizes instrumental ties: each party attempts to maintain a constant ratio between what he or she puts into and gets out of the relationship. For example, a taxi driver and his passenger have such a tenuous, temporary relationship with one another, although it may not be viewed as a "tie" at first glance. Each has a goal, the one to earn a living, the other to arrive at a destination. Each bargains with the other in an impersonal manner. The affective component of such a relationship is extremely low.

   Instrumental ties are formed—and usually broken—whenever a non-Chinese interacts with a Chinese in a situation where service or other assistance is provided in either direction. But these ties do carry the potential of becoming closer over time. Knowledge of instrumental ties should enable you to behave appropriately so that relations can proceed smoothly and occasionally develop into friendships.

3. Mixed ties: This type of relationship combines aspects of the previous two. Mixed ties link people who know each other reasonably well, sometimes over many years; there is a warm, emotional component to a mixed tie (though not as strong as in the case of an affective tie). Such relationships typically involve people in a durable, interpersonal network, based on shared past or present experience, of the type that easily forms in a society where there is relatively little mobility. Mixed ties are also instrumental because they enable people to attain practical ends. Resources are allocated back and forth according to

the equity rule: each party expects that over the long-term course of their relationship, giving and receiving will tend to balance. People having this type of relationship are said to have *guanxi*.

Guanxi relationships are important to the Chinese because of their affective component, their durability, and their functional value. Understanding this type of relationship is vital because it is the type in which you are most likely to become involved on an ongoing basis. Understanding the nature of guanxi and some of the cultural barriers that can inhibit the formation of good American-Chinese relationships should help you establish and maintain mixed ties that are cooperative, warm, open, informal, respectful, trusting, communicative, and empathetic as well as functional (instrumental) in the practical sense.

Chinese-Style Relationships and Their Pitfalls for Americans

Though little research has been done to compare and contrast the relationship patterns that are typical of the United States and the PRC, we know of four specific differences that may create unexpected barriers for the American who wishes to establish and maintain good relations with the Chinese. In this section we offer suggestions regarding these differences: formality expectations, guanxi connections, harmonious interactions, and friendship obligations.

Formality Expectations

A problem often faced by Americans beginning a relationship with a Chinese concerns levels of formality. Early in social relationships, the Chinese act in a relatively formal manner toward each other. In so doing, they show respect for each other's place in the established hierarchy and ensure that their contact will proceed harmoniously.

Social life in the United States tends to lack stability because mobility, both social and geographic, is one of the principal characteristics of Americans. Highly mobile individuals are less likely to feel bound by an ethos of hierarchy and harmony. Their lives are more likely to be guided by internal motives than by social structure. In this context, formality has little practical usefulness. The informality that pervades social life in the United States enables Americans to act freely, competing with one another and paying little attention to hierarchical patterns (which are only temporarily applicable in any case).

Although those Chinese who have had no previous experience working with Americans may at first be taken aback by their informality, the major problem is not simply that Americans fail to act in a formal manner. The Chinese are not necessarily offended by the discovery that a newly met American is exuberant, smiles a lot, and fails to use the customary formal styles of address.

The major problem is more subtle. As a Chinese gradually establishes a friendship with another Chinese, their formality dissolves very slowly into informality, which is a nonverbal affirmation that the two acquaintances are deepening their relationship into something closer and more durable. Accordingly, when an American acts in an informal fashion at the very beginning of a relationship, a Chinese is led to believe that the American intends to leap over the usual formal preliminaries in order to form a close, durable relationship without delay. That is rarely the American's intent. The outcome may be that within the subsequent few weeks, the Chinese experiences acute disappointment and feels critical of the American for being ungenuine and superficial.

It is likely that you personally subscribe to a typically American assumption about human relations: formality is associated with emotional coolness and distance, and informality is associated with emotional warmth and closeness. This assumption does not have validity among the Chinese.

Formality-informality on the one hand and emotional warmth-coolness on the other hand are not inextricably linked but often vary independently of each other. Chinese formality actually signals positive, friendly regard for you. From the Chinese point of view, to treat you informally early in the relationship would be to treat you shabbily.

Guanxi Connections

The word *guanxi* has no precise English equivalent, but it does have connotations that can be expressed in English: relationship, connection, obligation, and dependency. Guanxi is often spoken of as something linking two people who in some way have developed a relationship of mutual dependence. The Chinese gain leverage in daily affairs through guanxi, which enables them to call upon certain others to supply, or to assist in gaining access to, scarce goods and services. In some cases, the flow of scarce goods and services tends to be largely in one direction.[2] More often, however, the relationship involves an ongoing series of reciprocal exchanges. One gives to another and therefore expects, at some unspecified future date, to receive from that other person. Or, if one receives, one incurs an obligation to give later on. What is received need not be similar to what was given: one's gift of imported wine may later be repaid by the other's use of influence with a local policeman to waive a fine. Giving in the guanxi system is a kind of social investment upon which one may draw later.

For example, if you want to start a joint-venture factory in a coastal city in China and you need to put up some buildings, normally you need to go through about a dozen offices of different government departments for permission to build. This will take up to several months in addition to all the frustrations and setbacks you are likely to suffer in the process. But if you happen to be friendly with someone who has good connections (or good guanxi) with government officials, your experience is likely to be quite different. You will have the green light all the way, and your time to complete the project will be cut drastically. Your friend will introduce you to officials and others who are influential in making decisions about constructing buildings, and they in turn will help you to get around the hurdles and otherwise simplify and speed the process.

Guanxi relationships are informal and unofficial, but they are not a cold and calculating exchange.[3] The development of guanxi converts a person who was merely an acquaintance into a type of ingroup member, then uses the ongoing exchanges of favors as the means of maintaining the relationship. In other words, what is given and received are tokens that the personal side of the relationship is alive and well. A Chinese has guanxi relations with all sorts of people: clerks in local shops, work unit colleagues, subordinates and supervisors, local officials, in-laws and relatives, and foreign colleagues and acquaintances.

No one who is routinely living or working among the Chinese can decide to remain wholly outside of the guanxi system. Any act of helpfulness or generosity, no matter whether given or received, begins to draw one into the network of reciprocal exchanges. And no one should wish to remain wholly outside the guanxi system, because it not only is the "grease" that makes much of daily life run smoothly but is also one of the chief means whereby a foreigner can begin to build positive personal relationships with ordinary Chinese people.

But the guanxi system has pitfalls for foreigners. One is that they have little sense of the level of giving and receiving that is appropriate for any given mixed-tie relationship. Gifts or favors of different values are appropriate for people at different levels in the hierarchy and for people at different stages in a relationship. Problems may arise if a non-Chinese gives or receives a gift or favor that is viewed as unusually large or small by the Chinese person involved. For example, if you were to accept from a Chinese a gift or favor that he or she viewed as unusually valuable, you would incur a heavy obligation to repay in some way or another. You would probably not be fully aware of the extent of this obligation and even less aware of when and how your guanxi partner might expect that obligation to be discharged. (Guanxi cannot be equated with bribery, which all non-Chinese should shun assiduously.)

Sometimes awareness of the extent of one's obligation comes too late. For example, a Chinese who feels she has given a lot to you might decide that a suitable repayment would be for you to assist her in gaining entry to the United States and finding employment with an American company. Since you probably lack sufficient influence to make good on such a request and since you may also have no inclination to use your influence in that way, your Chinese friend must face deep disappointment. In such a case, the Chinese may signal her displeasure by abruptly terminating the relationship.

The Chinese tend to assume that something similar to the guanxi system operates in the United States[4] and that you are a part of it. Carrying this one step further, they assume that if you are influential enough to have a respected, well-paying job, then you must be influential enough to pull the strings necessary to bring about whatever they desire.

You cannot prevent your Chinese acquaintances from making false assumptions about obligation networks in American society, and you cannot prevent them from trying to arrange to study or work in the States. What you can do, however, is avoid giving them any reason to believe you can guarantee that they will attain their objectives through your intervention. Never promise more than you can deliver. Never imply that you have the ability to deliver. Will you write letters of recommendation? Perhaps yes. But don't let your Chinese friends believe that your recommendations will ensure acceptances.

Guanxi does not make it impossible for the Chinese to act on the basis of spontaneous feelings. You need not become obsessed about strings being attached to every little gift and favor you receive. But you should be suspicious in the unlikely event that a Chinese friend or acquaintance offers you a valuable gift. This gesture, no matter how spontaneous it may seem, has a very high probability of signaling that a major favor will be expected from you in the future.[5]

Harmonious Interactions

In a culture where individualism is as highly valued as it is in the United States, people are expected to take the initiative in advancing their personal interests and well-being and to be direct and assertive in interacting with others. High social and geographic mobility and the comparatively superficial nature of many personal attachments create a climate where interpersonal competition and a modest level of abrasiveness are tolerated and even expected.

The situation among the Chinese is different. Personal relations are predicated on the assumption that intragroup harmony should be conspicuously preserved at all costs. The limited social and geographic mobility in China and the deep and durable nature of many Chinese relationships create a situation in which abrasiveness is condemned and personal assertiveness is branded as selfish and is roundly criticized.

A little background on the Chinese word *gerenzhuyi* might be helpful in clarifying this issue. Gerenzhuyi is literally translated as "one person doctrine" but is commonly used to mean both "individualism" and "selfishness." In traditional Chinese culture, an individual's talents were not allowed to develop freely. A young Chinese grew up expecting to serve his or her father and the emperor. To those who showed more than a tiny tendency to follow their own predilections, social sanctions brought swift and inevitable punishment. During the late 1950s, attacks on any manifestation of individual assertiveness or personal ambition became especially severe and were intensified during the Cultural Revolution. In that political climate, gerenzhuyi became an all-purpose pejorative (much as "communist" was in the United States during the McCarthy era). In terms of popular attitude, nongroup-oriented behavior of any kind was not tolerated. Even though the Cultural Revolution was over by the late 1970s, sensitivity on the matter of gerenzhuyi continues among older Chinese.

Most Americans view self-promoting behavior as acceptable, if not necessarily laudable, so long as the interests and rights of others are not directly infringed upon. But most Chinese lose their equanimity when they encounter Americans who are direct and assertive in seeking their own personal advantage. To the Chinese, such behavior is a threat to intragroup harmony. Americans are concerned about the actual effects of individualistic behavior on others; Chinese focus on the potential damage to group harmony that individualistic behavior might cause.

The Chinese point of view on these matters manifests itself in subtle ways. For example, some Chinese may prove incapable of understanding why an American friend prefers to spend the evening alone. For an individual to want to spend time alone is perfectly acceptable among Americans, but it is viewed as a threat to group harmony by the Chinese, who equate aloneness with loneliness and who have no word for privacy in the American sense.

One behavior that the Chinese will not tolerate is anger. An angry person undermines the dignity and well-being of the group and is not considered worthy of respect, thus suffering a serious loss of face. Whether the anger is justifiable does not enter into their thinking. Americans understand that anger can seriously upset group harmony. But they are prepared to tolerate anger—if it is justified—as a dimension of self-expression, something Americans value highly.

The story is told of an American woman in China who, upon arrival, was told apologetically that her living quarters were not yet fully prepared. She would have to sleep in an unused kitchen. She was unhappy, of course, but she handled the situation with outward calm for a week, then for another week, and then for a third. But after a month with no change, she exploded in rage. From an American point of view, she was justified. In China, however, the provocation did not justify her anger. The remainder of her sojourn was ruined. None of her Chinese colleagues would cooperate with her and she returned early to the United States.

What should she have done? She should have reacted firmly (but without anger) on the day of her arrival, saying unequivocally that the unused kitchen was not suitable. She should have requested repeatedly to discuss the matter with top administrators; she should not have relented until she was able to have such a discussion and to get assigned to more suitable (if not necessarily ideal) quarters. By accepting the kitchen as her quarters for nearly a month, she gave the impression that it was minimally acceptable to her, thus ensuring that the Chinese would be perplexed as well as deeply offended by her eventual rage.

Friendship Obligations

Forming a close Chinese-American friendship, an affective tie, is not terribly difficult. But maintaining a friendship that is fully satisfactory to the Chinese partner may be difficult for Americans, whose expectations of friendship differ from those of the Chinese. Americans who wish to establish friendships with the Chinese are seeking admittance to one of the other person's ingroups (in this case, a group of close friends), just as they would when establishing a friendship in the United States. But as soon as the American becomes clearly identified by the Chinese as an ingroup member, the expectations of the Chinese partner regarding the extent of their mutual dependence vastly increase. Many Americans, especially men, are not prepared for such a high level of mutual dependence outside the context of their nuclear families.

Americans who have had little experience in cultures with highly interdependent friendship patterns may object to the foregoing analysis. It may seem to them that friends in the United States do depend upon one another in a way that is emotionally meaningful and practically useful. But "old China hands," anthropologists, and even Americans who have lived in China for only a few months all notice a fundamental difference that can be described as follows.

In the United States, a person usually has numerous friends at any one time, but these friends gradually change over the years. One's friends tend not to share all aspects of one's life but rather to be linked to specific activities (golfing partners, drinking buddies, professional colleagues, jogging companions, bridge foursomes, and so forth). Even one's best friends (the few toward whom one feels the greatest emotional attachment and in whom one is most likely to confide) may change several times as the decades roll by. More important, one's duties and obligations toward best friends are understood to have limits; one does not expect friends, even best friends, to assume burdensome, long-term responsibilities toward oneself. A close friend in the United States is a person that one feels free to ask for help, recognizing, however, that the friend is free to decline for cause. This general pattern is especially true of American men; American women tend to accept a greater degree of mutual dependence in their close friendships.

In China, a person has a limited number of friends, but these are close friends with whom one maintains a relationship throughout the course of a lifetime. One may add friends, but one rarely allows a friendship to wither and die. A person's friends, though few in number, share most aspects of his or her life. The duties and obligations of friendship are virtually unlimited for all practical purposes. One has enormous responsibility for one's friends; conversely, one expects to be able to rely heavily on one's friends. A friend in China is someone who, sensing that you are in need in some way, offers to assist you without waiting to be asked. You are also free to tell a friend what he or she must do in order to assist or please you. This pattern of friendship tends to characterize both males and females in China.

Before committing yourself too deeply to a friendship with a Chinese, ask yourself these questions.

1. Am I willing to spend a very high proportion of my nonfamily, nonwork time with the same individual? For example, if my Chinese friend routinely wanted to spend much of every Saturday, Sunday, and holiday with me, would I agree to this happily?

2. Am I able to accept frequent unscheduled visiting by the same individual? For example, if my Chinese friend often showed up at my door, sometimes early in the morning or late at night, could I avoid feeling that my privacy was being invaded?

3. Am I ready to be asked for favors frequently by the same person or to be told what I should be doing for him or her? For example, if my Chinese friend often expected to use items that I viewed as valued private property, would I comply without protest?

4. Can I accept frequent advice and caretaking behavior from the same person? For example, if my Chinese friend often made critical comments about my style of dressing, would I be able to accept this without feeling that my adult independence was being impugned?

5. Can I feel comfortable with a considerable amount of physical contact from a friend who is a member of the same sex? For example, if my Chinese friend expected to walk hand in hand with me on some occasions, would I feel that this was reasonable and proper? (This question applies to young men as well as young women.)

If you find it difficult to answer yes wholeheartedly to most of the above questions, you should think twice about trying to establish a truly close friendship with a Chinese person.[6]

Some Cautionary Advice about Romance

Some Americans fall in love with a Chinese man or woman, get married, and (sometimes) live happily ever after. Yet, cautionary words are in order. The reason is not that the process of establishing a romantic attachment with a Chinese is difficult. On the contrary, it is too easy.

Courtship practices among Americans are based on the assumption that it is right and good for a young person to be involved in a series of romantic attachments over several years before finally settling into marriage. This assumption is the basis for dating, going steady, and even living together. The rationale for serial romances is that one will be far better able to make the choice of a long-term partner if one has had previous experiences with a range of temporary partners. Since the sexual revolution of the 1960s, Americans' romances have often included sexual relations.

This typically American set of assumptions does not operate in the culture of the Chinese. Furthermore, these assumptions have a high potential for getting Americans into great difficulty. The Chinese most emphatically do not share the idea that wide experience of any sort with members of the opposite sex is a desirable precursor to long-term commitment. Any young person who is seen as sharing his or her affections with a series of others is viewed thereafter as an undesirable romantic partner, someone that serious, responsible members of the opposite sex had better avoid. Although this attitude is beginning to change, it remains strongly ingrained in many Chinese.

Just as same-sex friendships are virtually always maintained for life among the Chinese, so are heterosexual attachments. Once a romantic relationship is acknowledged, it is expected by the partners' acquaintances as well as by the partners themselves to be permanent. Romantic physical contact of any sort is an acknowledgment of strong attachment. This includes not only sexual intercourse but also kissing, petting, and hugging. Even mere hand-holding conveys serious romantic intent among traditional-thinking Chinese.

The danger in Chinese-American romances is that the American, acting on typical American assumptions, will demonstrate affection for his or her Chinese friend by a physical act of endearment. This may be one that, to the American, seems quite innocent of deep meaning, such as kissing. It may be accompanied by a verbal expression of affection that also carries no deep meaning for the American. But acts such as these usually send a clear message to the Chinese, which may be paraphrased as "This is the love of my life!" Instant bonding may result.

Most Americans are terrified when they discover that the person with whom they thought they were having a casual if affectionate date is now eager to discuss the course of their lives together. They are mortified when they find that their efforts to extricate themselves, albeit gently, result in major psychological trauma and perhaps even the involvement of Chinese relatives incensed at the idea that the respectability of a family member is about to be forever tarnished.

Of course, the American may seriously intend a permanent attachment leading to marriage. If so, the Chinese partner's family members may be pleased about this—but not necessarily. Traditionally, the Chinese have had a deep fear of miscegenation. And the distrust of foreigners engendered by historical episodes of foreign occupation as well as by indoctrination during the Cultural Revolution still lingers in the minds of some. So the prospect of marriage to a non-Chinese person may bring threats of disownment from parents. The Chinese partner to such a marriage may be stigmatized by friends. The leaders of the person's work unit also may disapprove, a matter that cannot be ignored in China. So the American who contemplates marriage to a Chinese would be wise to determine the extent, if any, to which objections may arise before taking any unalterable steps.

Finally, we offer two important notes of caution. Since

China began opening to the outside world, prostitution has emerged in the coastal cities. Tourists and businessmen staying at hotels sometimes receive calls from young women offering sexual services. We strongly advise against using these services. Prostitution and the use of prostitutes are criminal offenses in the PRC. There are cases of foreign businessmen who, because they became involved with prostitutes, landed in jail, were victims of blackmail, or had confidential documents stolen from their hotel rooms.

Homosexuality is viewed by the vast majority of Chinese as a low and contemptible practice. A charge of homosexuality can ruin the life of a Chinese, even to the point of his or her being banished forever from contact with family and friends. Do not expect any Chinese to accept this overwhelming risk.

---

[1] Michael Harris Bond and Kwang-kuo Hwang, "'The Social Psychology of the Chinese People," in *The Psychology of the Chinese People*, edited by Michael Harris Bond (Hong Kong: Oxford University Press, 1986), 223–26. Some of the information we give with respect to affective, instrumental, and mixed ties is quoted from this source, but much is paraphrased. We have substituted the term *affective ties* for Hwang's original term, *expressive ties*.

[2] Regarding unidirectional *guanxi*, Lucian Pye says,

> In a guanxi relationship one party can repeatedly press for favors, or, as the Chinese express it, *la guanxi*, that is, "pull guanxi." Since the core element of guanxi is not reciprocity but a particularism [based, for example, on a common background factor such as origin in the same village or attendance at the same school], and since guanxi can quite properly be used for material advantage, a party seeking benefits can repeatedly ask for favors from the more advantaged party without making any explicit sacrifices in return. It is only necessary for the party seeking the favor to appeal to established rules of propriety and to try to shame the other into acting for him.

Lucian W. Pye, *Asian Power and Politics: The Cultural Dimensions of Authority* (Cambridge: Belknap Press, 1985), 295; material in brackets is abstracted from p. 293.

[3] Regarding the warm human feelings that are potentially a part of guanxi, Pye makes the following observation:

> The basis of guanxi is not deeply internalized sensitivities and compulsions. Guanxi relationships can, however, be greatly strengthened by *ganqing*, which...does not exactly mean "sentiments," "feelings," or "emotion" but is nevertheless the "affective component" of guanxi. If the ganqing is "good" then the guanxi will be "close." Ganqing is neither friendship nor moral obligation. It is the quality of a relationship that is premised to a substantial degree on common interests.

Pye, *Asian Power and Politics*, 293.

[4] This assumption is true to some extent, of course, but in an individualistic culture such as that of the United States, personal influence is limited by considerations of objectivity and universalism, whereas in a collectivist culture such as China, personal influence is promoted by the emphasis on subjectivity and particularism.

[5] For an extended discussion of guanxi, see Mayfair Mei-hui Yang, *Gifts, Favors and Banquets: The Art of Social Relationships in China* (Ithaca: Cornell University Press, 1994).

[6] An acquaintance of ours notes that he has occasionally encountered Chinese people in the PRC who act in a manner quite different from the generalizations we have stated in this section. On those occasions, a young Chinese has straightforwardly said, "Let's be friends" or "Can we be friends?" within only five or ten minutes of first meeting him. Assuming that one is not inclined to agree to a friendship on such short notice, what should one do in such a case? The challenge is to decline the Chinese person's invitation while allowing him or her to maintain face. We think you should take "the cultural line," which in this case would lead you to say that as a typical American, you are not accustomed to agreeing to friendships on short acquaintance.

Thank the Chinese person for wanting to be friends and, if you can, be complimentary regarding his or her English. But stress that the American way of life simply does not prepare you to form friendships in this manner.

8

八

Education and Training among the Chinese

Teaching and Training the Chinese Today

After a few sessions as observers or presenters in a room full of students or trainees in China, American business trainers as well as academics and teachers often comment on how reluctant the members of the audience are to make direct contributions of any kind to the proceedings. This tends to be true even among graduate students and adult professional trainees (although professional trainees with prior experience in American firms might be more talkative). Chinese students and trainees usually present themselves as an attentive, respectful, and, above all, passive audience. They arrive, they listen, they take copious notes, they depart. Even when invited to make comments or ask questions, they are reluctant to speak. The disinclination of Chinese trainees and students to express their personal opinions frustrates American and other Western presenters, who characteristically hope to encourage informal discussions and "Q&A" sessions during their classes, seminars, or training events.

Their hopes are not entirely in vain, however. During

breaks and at the end of the class or workshop, some attendees commonly speak with the professor or trainer. These
impromptu question-and-answer sessions occasionally turn
into vigorous and lengthy exchanges of views. Therefore, the
wise trainer or teacher will plan ahead for the possibility of
remaining in the classroom for at least half an hour after his
or her formal presentation has concluded.

Besides the fact that Chinese educational tradition places
no value on self-expression by students or trainees, the following more practical reasons are sometimes given by individual audience members for their disinclination to speak.
Poor learners usually say they are afraid of losing face if they
speak, since they might say something stupid. Outstanding
learners usually say they fear being looked upon as show-offs
by their classmates (also creating loss of face) if they speak
too often or say things that are obviously brilliant. Average
learners seem to have the least reluctance to speak; they say,
however, that there is no point in their speaking unless they
have something really valuable to contribute. Few Chinese
share the assumption of most American trainers and teachers
that audience participation has intrinsic value. In the students' and trainees' view, run-of-the-mill discussions waste
precious time that ought to be used by the teacher or trainer
to deliver intellectual treasures to the audience.

Longer acquaintance with Chinese classroom practices and
with the habits and preferences of Chinese students and
teachers will reveal many, if not all, of the following tendencies.

1. The transmission of knowledge is oriented more toward
   theory than toward practice and application. The preferred mode of thinking is deductive, not inductive or
   operational as it is in the United States.[1]

2. Great emphasis is placed on details and facts, which are
   often committed to memory. Americans worry little about
   remembering facts; instead, they focus on knowing where
   to find facts and how to use them creatively. The Chinese

are uncomfortable with the American tendency to deemphasize factual recall.[2]

3. A key learning objective is to know and be able to state facts and theories as givens, as wholes. Chinese students are rarely able to employ an analytical conceptual style, which Americans value.[3]

4. The content of learning is whatever is found in assigned texts or other readings; books are the sources of authority. Using books merely as sources of opinions or interpretations, as American teachers often do, is not understood or appreciated by the students.[4]

5. The teachers whose classroom style is most admired are those who give clearly structured, information-packed lectures with much information written on the blackboard (which students copy verbatim). Experiential learning, problem solving, case studies, and participatory teaching methods are distrusted and may be resisted.[5]

6. Tests are extremely important because, like the imperial examinations of old, they are viewed as the absolute determinants of a student's future. Chinese students do not understand that American teachers use tests primarily to gauge a student's progress.[6]

Chinese students also prefer a teacher who deals with various topics in a manner that might be called "by the numbers." Suppose a teacher is discussing the origins of American individualism. She should start with a heading (say, "The Five Precursors of Individualism in the United States"), clearly list the five precursors with numbers and brief headings, then discuss each in turn. If she writes all the headings on the blackboard, so much the better. If she rambles while trying to interrelate everything she is saying, so much the worse.

Chinese students hold books and other written materials in awe, but most will resist long (more than one hundred pages) reading assignments. They may also try to bargain regarding their length and sometimes about other things, too, including their grades. The explanation for this behavior is that they study with great intensity and seriousness of purpose, and in many cases memorize page after page of text, so that the prospect of long assignments is positively overwhelming.[7] An additional explanation that applies at Chinese universities is that there are severe limits on students' access to books.

A typical strategy of American university teachers is to lecture on some aspects of their course subject but expect other aspects to be covered by the assigned readings. Chinese students are not accustomed to this practice. They expect teachers to cover the assigned readings at length during the lectures. Therefore, a careful explanation and rationale are called for if a teacher intends to do things in the typical American fashion.

Laughter in classrooms, as in many other social contexts in Chinese culture, can have a variety of meanings, only one of which is that something genuinely humorous has been said or done. When laughter erupts in a classroom, either from an individual or from part or all of the group, it may be masking an uncomfortable situation by making it seem lighthearted. If a young woman is called upon to recite or answer a question and she giggles—women tend to giggle instead of laugh—she may be too embarrassed to answer. And if Chinese students laugh unexpectedly at a point made by a foreign teacher, perhaps he or she has touched on a topic that creates anxiety for the students.[8]

American professors (especially those in the humanities and social sciences) often give essay tests on which they expect their students to discuss an issue from several points of view; typically, such tests are graded not on the basis of right and wrong answers but rather of command of information and quality of reasoning. American teachers also abhor plagiarism. These attitudes can lead to misunderstandings with Chinese students, who may repeat verbatim on a test something previously read (and memorized) in the belief that this is a widely approved way to attain a high mark. The issue of plagiarism does not arise in the minds of most Chinese students.

American teachers often write messages to students on the tests or essays that they are grading; they assume that these messages are private communications. But sometimes Chinese students show each other their graded tests and essays so that their answers and the teacher's comments can be compared. Therefore, a teacher ought not to write anything that is not suitable for public consumption. Private communication with Chinese students is best done verbally.

Student Life and Relationships in the PRC

Student life at Chinese universities has its unpleasant aspects. Students live in barren, concrete-floored dormitories. The furniture and possessions of four or six or even eight students must fit into one room roughly the size of a large walk-in pantry. On most campuses the students are expected to bring their own bowls and utensils to the dining hall (which means that they must wash them after eating), to fetch and carry the hot water to do their laundry (which is washed by hand and dried on outdoor lines), to get by with very limited access to libraries, and to study under inadequate lighting after dark.

But in spite of material hardships, they do learn. Furthermore, there are diversions of various kinds. Some students still take wushui, the nap after lunch. An hour in the late afternoon is reserved on many campuses for informal sports activities, such as Ping-Pong, volleyball, badminton, and even Frisbee. Motion pictures are shown (usually outdoors) twice a week on most campuses and are very popular. Class outings occur occasionally in the spring and fall.

The pattern of social relationships among Chinese students tends to be strikingly different from that common among students in the United States. Americans are quite likely to be acquainted, and even to make friends, with a wide cross-section of fellow students. This pattern is the natural outcome of the freedom each student has to determine his or her roommates, place of residence, academic courses, academic schedule, and extracurricular activities. This pattern is a natural outcome of individualism as a value system.

Chinese students are tightly integrated into small groups; the principal groups for most students are their roommates and their classmates (involving fifteen to twenty others, occasionally up to fifty others). By classmates we mean the students who go together as a group from class to class. Since there is relatively little choice of courses for Chinese students, their academic schedules are largely determined on a group basis. These class collectives are often stable over the three or four years that the students spend at the institution. (These characteristics of Chinese universities are in the process of changing. An increasing number of courses are becoming available, and students are gaining more opportunity to pursue their individual interests by varying their schedules from that of their collective.)

Of course, there are numerous other students at the institution, including those who entered in the same year and will graduate simultaneously. In the United States, students in the same year or class (as in the "class of 1992") have a fairly strong identity with each other, but this is not necessarily the case in China. A Chinese student at a large university has little social contact with those who entered the institution simultaneously, even less with those who entered at other times.[9] His or her social life is intensely focused on roommates and members of the class collective. This pattern is a natural outcome of collectivism as a value system.

Classmates in China are not simply a conglomeration of young people who develop deep relationships with each other; they are also a social unit with leadership. The leader is the class monitor, who is elected by his or her peers. (Other, lesser leaders are also elected to look after specific aspects of the class collective's life.) Class monitors feel responsible for their classmates and are not averse to giving them pointed advice about their social behavior. When the class has an activity such as an outing together, it is the monitor who sees that it is properly organized and carried out.

The monitor also serves as the spokesperson for the class in its dealings with institutional officials and individual faculty members. In fact, a conscientious monitor will give a professor advice about how to be more effective in dealing with the class collective. Such advice might concern the scheduling of examinations, the quantity of homework, or even the methods employed in class by the professor. American professors in China should not be taken aback when a monitor offers advice. It is more appropriate to be grateful for this institutionalized way of receiving frank communication from the students via their designated intermediary.

Competitive behavior can sometimes be observed among Chinese students, but it is more likely to be found in secondary schools (middle schools) because of the extremely limited number of university places. When competition is seen among university students, it is often caused by the scarcity of certain resources such as books and other kinds of printed materials. Cutthroat competition (such as deliberately keeping assigned readings from circulating) is not often a feature of Chinese student life.[10]

There are conflicting reports on how diligently students in China apply themselves to their studies. Those who view students as strongly motivated note that they can be seen studying late into the night or rehearsing their recitations at the crack of dawn. They are also capable of accurately memorizing large quantities of material, such as foreign language vocabulary lists or whole chapters of textbooks.

Those who view Chinese students as lacking motivation often point to the so-called "iron rice bowl" policy, which says that all students who enter an institution of higher education are guaranteed employment (though not necessarily that of their own choosing) upon graduation. But government policy has recently changed. Beginning with those students who entered in 1989, there is no longer a guarantee of employment or assignment of jobs; instead, students will be interviewed and their academic record scrutinized by prospective employers.

There is some justification for both views. The PRC has an educational system that progressively strips away large numbers of ordinary and low achievers while rewarding those who do especially well. Students whose academic work has been of the highest quality are funneled toward a few outstanding colleges and universities. Observers at those particular institutions tend to conclude that Chinese students are exceptionally diligent; observers at other institutions tend to reach a variety of less laudable conclusions.

The Special Role of Chinese Teachers

The Chinese word for a teacher at any level, *laoshi,* is not merely a designation of social rank and function but a term signifying considerable respect and deference. Perhaps the greatest difference between Chinese laoshi and American professors is the quality of the relationships they tend to have with their students. It is not unheard-of for American professors to form close relationships with their students, but this usually means that the two have developed an informal way of interacting in which they view each other less and less in superior-subordinate roles. In China, closeness between laoshi and student does not usually involve informality or a lessening of deference and respect on the part of the student. Among the Chinese, respectful formality and polite correctness are not viewed as inimical to a caring relationship.

Likewise, it is not unheard-of for American professors and teachers to act occasionally as mentors to students. Consistent with the emphasis on self-reliance in an individualistic culture, however, these mentor relationships are rarely characterized by the teacher's playing a parental role vis-à-vis the student. So in those rather uncommon instances where an American teacher acts as a mentor to a student over an extended period of time, the focus of the teacher's advice and counsel tends to be limited to their mutual professional or academic concerns; rarely does it cross over into such personal areas as the student's social, political, physical, and moral development.

But in China, a laoshi is expected to take a strong interest in the development of each student as a whole person. To a remarkable extent, the laoshi role overlaps that of the student's parents. In China, the role of a laoshi is said to be *jiaoshu yüren*, which is literally translated "to teach book [and] to educate (nurture, bring up, rear) people." The second portion of this role, yüren, implies bringing up youth to be socially minded, a very broad educational goal by American standards.

The laoshi role is humorously depicted by Mark Salzman in his account of the two years he spent in the People's Republic. Salzman was very young when he went to the city of Changsha as an English teacher at a medical college. He describes the following encounter.

> My [Chinese] lessons with Teacher Wei had come to involve more than reading and writing assignments. She was a teacher in the Chinese tradition, taking responsibility not only for my academic progress but for my development as a person. She had advice for me concerning my family and friends, my diet, my clothing, my study and exercise habits, and my attitude toward life. At times I got impatient with her and explained that in America, children become adults around the time they leave for college and like to make decisions for themselves after that. She was appalled. "Don't your parents and teachers care about you?"
>
> "Of course they do, but—"

"Then how can they leave you stranded when you are only a child?"

"Well, we—"

"And how can you possibly think you understand everything? You are only twenty-two years old! You are so far away from home, and I am your teacher; if I don't care about you, won't you be lonely?"

She pointed out that the close relationship between teacher and student has existed in China since before the time of Confucius and should not be underestimated—besides, she was older than me and knew better. I couldn't help respecting her conviction, and she seemed to get such pleasure out of trying to figure and then to straighten me out that I stopped resisting and let her educate me.

I learned how to dress to stay comfortable throughout the year (a useful skill in a place without air-conditioning or heat in most buildings), how to prevent and treat common illness, how to behave toward teachers, students, strangers, and bureaucrats, how to save books from mildew and worms, and never to do anything to excess.

"Mark, you laugh a great deal during your lectures. Why?"

"Because, Teacher Wei, I am having fun."

"I see. Laugh less. It seems odd that a man laughs so hard at his own jokes. People think you are a bit crazy, or perhaps choking."

"Teacher Wei, do you think it is bad to laugh?"

"No, not at all. In fact, it is healthy to laugh. In Chinese we have a saying that if you laugh you will live long. But you shouldn't laugh too much, or you will have digestive problems."[11]

We emphasize this point about the accountability that Chinese teachers feel for their students for good reason. If you are teaching Chinese students, some of them may expect you to be concerned about more than just their intellectual and professional growth, which may cause you to chafe under the weight of their dependence. As an American, you have learned to accept as natural the assumption that the overtly dependent aspects of relationships should be minimized as much as possible. You have learned to value self-reliance not only in yourself but also in others.

The Traditions of American and Chinese Education[12]

According to the traditional policies and practices of Chinese education, students are taught that they must fit harmoniously into the overall scheme of human relations, a scheme in which awareness of the group takes strong precedence over the desires of the individual and in which emphasis is given to the beneficial aspects of hierarchical relationships. Since any person's place in the family and community hierarchy is largely determined by age, enormous importance is placed on the way things are done by the oldest people, who in turn revere the way things were done by those already deceased. Given these values, schools operating in the Chinese tradition focus their curriculum heavily on writings from the past, writings treated more or less as sacred texts worthy of being committed to memory. The objectives of this curriculum are moral and normative: to transform the young into people with a highly developed social conscience and to inculcate in them the code for living already accepted by their elders.

Given this moral focus of education, the relationship between student and teacher, as we have seen, necessarily goes beyond the transmission of information. The teacher is an instructor, of course, but also an educator in that he or she prepares the student for all aspects of life as a socially aware and responsible member of the community and a citizen of the nation. Chinese teachers feel personally accountable for their students' overall development as human beings. Note, however, that this feeling does not lead to what Americans would call individualized instruction or student-centered learning.

The policies and practices of education in the contemporary United States could hardly be more different from those described above. Students are encouraged to follow their individual interests and to view themselves as distinct from the various groups to which they belong. It is not accurate to say that American classroom practices undermine community-mindedness or cooperation, but they do emphasize self-expression, self-reliance, self-motivation, individual initiative, and personal achievement. These emphases are grounded in a national educational policy that stresses equal educational opportunity for every person, regardless of background, economic level, or native ability. The basic purpose of American education is to prepare each individual to be able to attain his or her potential within existing political, social, and economic structures. Although the possibility that those structures can be improved is not ruled out, the focus is clearly on enabling the individual to thrive and be successful within society as it exists. The focus of American education is not moral but rather intensely practical.

---

[1] Deduction as a mode of thinking begins with first principles or axioms, which are customarily givens, then uses the techniques of logic to reason "downward" to derivative propositions, which, because they contain no inferences and no new information, are certain to be true so long as the given first principles are true. Induction as a mode of thinking begins with empirically verifiable facts and statistics, then reasons "upward" to conclusions or theories, which are treated as tentative because inferences are likely to have been used and because more facts and statistics may become available at any time. Operational thinking is a type of induction in which the basic objective is not to gain knowledge for its own sake but rather to learn information and skills in order to promote practical operations in the real world.

[2] Helen Young, "Cultural Differences between Chinese and

Americans" (Beijing: Foreign Experts' Bureau, n.d.), 1. She adds, "An American teacher often says, 'I don't know, but I will look it up for you.' Or 'I don't know but I can tell you where to find the information.'"

[3] Saying that the focus is on wholes is not to say that attention is denied to details. Rather it is to say that the details are assumed to be inextricably related to each other, to be inseparable. Analytical conceptual style, on the other hand, is concerned with the parts out of which wholes are made. Wholes are recognized as such, but the assumption is made that no whole can be properly or fully understood until it is broken down into its smallest constituent parts so that each part can be understood separately and its relation to each of the other parts can be understood as well. This process may be applied to the understanding of physical objects, statistical data, mental concepts, human behavior, or whatever. In discussing young Chinese teachers who had recently returned to Shanghai after studying in Canada, Tani E. Barlow and Donald M. Lowe wrote:

> Both Wang and Chen said that for them the most difficult part of Canadian university life was the examination requiring students to "analyze" a problem. It took them a full year, with the help of tutors, before they felt confident analyzing. Both felt exhilarated once they'd mastered it. As returned students, they told us, they feel it their duty to impart the skills of analysis and questioning to their own students and gradually lay the basis for a genuine modernization in education.

Tani E. Barlow and Donald M. Lowe, *Chinese Reflections: Americans Teaching in the People's Republic* (New York: Praeger, 1985), 152.

[4] Edgar A. Porter, "Foreign Involvement in China's Colleges and Universities: A Historical Perspective," *International Journal of Intercultural Relations* 11, no. 4 (1987): 380.

[5] Regarding a cadre training institute in the suburbs of Shanghai, Barlow and Lowe wrote:

> The language students tend to be even more conservative than the faculty. Ms. Wang said several told her to her face that they consider her "method" ridiculous and inappro-

priate. They refused to sit in a circle and speak English to each other. They don't like to invent conversations or play communication games. They insist on taking conventional exams. Several just don't attend her classes at all, preferring to audit the older professors' lectures on intensive reading and grammar instead. Since the older professors at the center don't care whether they speak English or not, all the students have to do is memorize twenty new vocabulary words a day and they can pass with flying colors.

Barlow and Lowe, *Chinese Reflections*, 151.

6   Porter, "Foreign Involvement in China's Colleges and Universities," 380–81.

7   While teaching in Beijing in 1986, the American author of this book attempted on several occasions to distinguish between sets of assigned readings that were worthy of concentrated attention and others that were to be read only for purposes of familiarization. He found the second set very largely ignored by the students. They seemed to assume that if a reading was not of critical importance, it did not deserve any attention whatsoever. (The students' habit of reading with enormous care was probably an outcome of an "intensive reading" course commonly given to foreign language students at most Chinese universities.)

8   The story is told of an American teacher who, exasperated for one reason or another, said to his class, "You are wasting your time and mine!" The students laughed and the teacher became all the more annoyed because he thought he was being ridiculed. Actually, the laughter was covering the students' acute embarrassment and shame at being so directly criticized.

9   At large Chinese universities drawing students from all over the nation, students from the same hometown or province maintain strong ties with one another. In such groups, the older students take the younger ones under their wing.

10   An acquaintance of ours who has taught in China observes that the eagerness of Chinese students to cooperate and share with one another probably accounts for their attitude toward what Americans would call cheating. In her experience, the line between sharing and cheating is blurred. She tells the story of two students, one of whom was the most gifted in one of her

courses, the other of whom was the weakest. They shared a desk in her classroom; they had been roommates as well as classmates for four years. The gifted one told her frankly that he allowed his friend to copy from his test paper because he would never be able to pass on his own. If he failed this course, he would not be able to graduate. There was no option to repeat the course, and no graduation meant no decent job. Said the gifted student, "It's my duty to help him."

[11] Mark Salzman, *Iron and Silk* (New York: Random House, 1986), 36–37.

[12] This discussion of the traditions of American and Chinese education owes much to the thinking of the late anthropologist Francis L. K. Hsu, as found in the section entitled "School," in *Americans and Chinese: Passage to Differences*, 3d ed. (Honolulu: The University Press of Hawaii, 1981), 92–108. For a useful discussion of the central moral thrust of Chinese education, see Jeffrey F. Meyer, "A Subtle and Silent Transformation: Moral Education in Taiwan and the People's Republic of China," in *The Revival of Values Education in Asia and the West*, edited by William K. Cummings et al. (Oxford, UK: Pergamon, 1988), especially pages 119–29. See also Edgar A. Porter, *Foreign Teachers in China: Old Problems for a New Generation, 1979-1989* (Westport, CT: Greenwood, 1990).

Additional Readings on Educational Practices among the Chinese

Items preceded by an asterisk are annotated in "Recommended Readings."

For a general overview of Chinese education and its contacts with the West in historical and organizational terms, consult the following.

Comparative Education 20, no. 1 (1984). This entire "Special Anniversary Number" focuses on education in China.

Porter, Edgar A. "Foreign Involvement in China's Colleges and Universities: A Historical Perspective." *International Journal of Intercultural Relations* 11, no. 4 (1987): 369–86.

Reed, Linda A. *Education in the People's Republic of China and U.S.-China Educational Exchanges*. Washington, DC: National Association for Foreign Student Affairs, 1988.

For practical information intended for educators and students who are (or soon will be) living and working in the People's Republic, consult the following.

Barlas, Robert. *The T.E.S.L.-Canada China Handbook*. Scarborough, Ontario: T.E.S.L.-Canada, 1985.

Hall, Christine. *Living & Working in China: How to Obtain Entry and Plan a Successful Stay*. Plymouth, UK: How To Books, 1996. See chapter 8, "Teaching English."

Parker, Jesse, and Janet Rodgers. *A Guide to Living, Studying, and Working in the People's Republic of China and Hong Kong*. rev. ed. New Haven, CT: Yale-China Association, 1986.

*Thurston, Anne F. *China Bound: A Guide to Academic Life and Work in the PRC*. rev. ed. Washington, DC: National Academy Press, 1994.

Watkins, David A., and John B. Biggs, eds. *The Chinese Learner: Cultural, Psychological, and Contextual Influences*. Hong Kong and Melbourne: Comparative Education Research Centre and The Australian Council for Educational Research, 1996.

Weiner, Rebecca, Margaret Murphy, and Albert Li. *Living in China: A Guide to Teaching and Studying in China Including Taiwan*. San Francisco: China Books & Periodicals, 1991.

For fascinating stories about the daily lives of Americans on Chinese university campuses, consult the following.

Barlow, Tani E., and Donald M. Lowe. *Chinese Reflections: Americans Teaching in the People's Republic*. New York: Praeger, 1985.

Leonard, Deborah. "A Walking Footnote: Teaching American and English Literature to Chinese Students." Occasional Papers in Intercultural Learning 11 (1986). Distributed by The AFS Center for the Study of Intercultural Learning, New York.

Miller, Marcia. "Reflections on Reentry after Teaching in China." Occasional Papers in Intercultural Learning 14 (1988). Distributed by The AFS Center for the Study of Intercultural Learning, New York.

Salzman, Mark. *Iron and Silk*. New York: Random House, 1986.

For an analysis of the fundamental cultural differences underlying the educational objectives and methods that are characteristic of the United States and the People's Republic, consult the following.

*Hsu, Francis L. K. *Americans and Chinese: Passage to Differences*, 3d ed. Honolulu: The University Press of Hawaii, 1981. See the section entitled "School," 92–108.

Porter, Edgar A. *Foreign Teachers in China: Old Problems for a New Generation, 1979-1989*. Westport, CT: Greenwood, 1990.

For some insight into what goes on in Chinese elementary and secondary schools, consult the following.

Grove, Cornelius L. "U.S. Schooling through Chinese Eyes." *Phi Delta Kappan* 65, 7 (March 1984): 481–82.

Hayhoe, Ruth, ed. *Contemporary Chinese Education*. Armonk, NY: M. E. Sharpe, 1984.

Kwong, Julia. "Changing Political Culture and Changing Curriculum: An Analysis of Language Textbooks in the People's Republic of China." *Comparative Education* 21, 2 (1985): 197–209.

Meyer, Jeffrey F. "A Subtle and Silent Transformation: Moral Education in Taiwan and the People's Republic of China," in *The Revival of Values Education in Asia and the West*, edited by William K. Cummings et al. Oxford, UK: Pergamon, 1988.

Tobin, Joseph J., David Y. H. Wu, and Dana H. Davidson. *Preschool in Three Cultures: Japan, China and the United States*. New Haven, CT: Yale University Press, 1989.

For additional information about education in the People's Republic of China, consult the following.

Garrott, June Rose. "Chinese Cultural Values: New Angles, Added Insights." *International Journal of Intercultural Relations* 19, no. 2 (1995): 211–25.

Jacobson, Robert L. "China's Campuses: Life Today May Often Be a Struggle, but Few Forget the Tougher Times Not Long Ago." *Chronicle of Higher Education*, 4 November 1987, 49–52.

94

*Pratt, Daniel D. "Conceptions of Self Within China and the United States: Contrasting Foundations for Adult Education." *International Journal of Intercultural Relations* 15, no. 3 (1991): 285–310.

Ragatz, Janet. "An Inside Look at University Living in Today's China." *Christian Science Monitor*, 9 November 1981, 19–20.

Thurston, Anne F., and Burton Pasternak, eds. *The Social Sciences and Fieldwork in China: Views from the Field*. Boulder, CO: Westview Press, 1983.

For information about the children of Western expatriates attending schools located in the PRC, consult the following.

Dakin, Julie A. "The ABCs of Going to School in China." *China Business Review* 16, no. 6 (November-December 1989): 44–47.

9

Negotiating and Institutional Decision Making*

Decision Making in Chinese Institutions

Decisions within Chinese institutions are usually arrived at through group process, whereas decisions in the United States are often associated with one individual. This difference is rather subtle. In Chinese governmental and institutional offices, as in American offices, some people carry more weight in the decision-making process than others. In both cases there is usually a leadership group consisting of the most powerful people who are likely to meet more or less regularly to keep themselves informed about what is going on and to discuss what ought to be done about current issues and problems. But in Chinese institutions, decisions are made by a process of leader-mediated compromise that involves people

---

* We have relied in the preparation of this chapter on the works recommended (at the end of this chapter) for additional reading. Our major source has been Lucian W. Pye, *Chinese Commercial Negotiating Style* (Cambridge, MA: Oelgeschlager, Gunn & Hain, 1982).

at several hierarchical levels discussing matters behind the scenes, circulating written memoranda, and meeting formally. By "leader-mediated compromise," we mean that the leader listens to the opinions of many people, then makes a decision that takes all opinions into account. The decision is not necessarily one that makes everyone equally happy or un-happy; it might favor one view (perhaps the leader's own view) over others. The value of harmony requires group members to "blend in" (*suihe*) at this point—but what they are blending in with is not precisely one another's opinions, but rather the final decision of their leader. In short, Chinese group members typically have more input in the decision-making process than do American group members. And a Chinese leader feels more obligated than an American leader to consider the views of numerous subordinates before he or she makes the final decision. One outcome of the Chinese way is that decision making requires a lot of time.

In the United States, even though several people may discuss various options and possibilities (especially when the principles of teamwork are being observed), decisions tend to be strongly identified with one individual. He or she is the person whose responsibilities are defined as including the issue or problem at hand. Also, many decisions in American institutions are made by a person who is at the middle level in the hierarchy; this mid-level person may confer with oth-ers at the same level, but not necessarily with top leaders, before making the decision. This individual-centered process does not guarantee better decisions than are made in China, but it does enable decisions to be made much more quickly.

A basic fact of institutional life in China is that decision making in most institutions operates under the jurisdiction and authority of governmental leaders at some level.[1] Control over institutional policies and activities emanates from the provincial capital or local seat of government if not from Beijing. Because of this top-down structure of guidance and control, decisions of any consequence must be referred for approval up the hierarchical ladder. There are hierarchical ladders in the United States, too, but they are shorter; approval, when necessary, is sought from one or two people at one's work site or at another location within one's institution.

Two typical frustrations of Americans who are working in or with Chinese institutions are (1) that they cannot determine who makes the decisions about the issue or problem on which they need action and (2) that they cannot get decisions made within a time frame that they believe is reasonable.[2] These frustrations are not based on mere misperceptions, for in Chinese institutions, responsibility is actually not focused on an individual but is diffused among members of a group. And because of the two procedures—consensus building and approval seeking—that must be observed, decisions actually do require much longer to finalize than is normally the case in the United States.[3]

The Cultural Bases of American and Chinese Decision Making

Institutional Decision-Making Values in the United States

Anthropologists and sociologists have long recognized that U.S. culture emphasizes individual initiative and personal achievement, making things work and getting things done, efficiency and timeliness of action, and making the lives of individuals more comfortable and convenient. These values are implicit in the American definition of success. Making money is a factor in success, too, but money (profit) is usually viewed as resulting from the accomplishment of worthwhile tasks in an efficient, effective, and productive manner.

Since accomplishing tasks is the paramount objective of most U.S. institutions, matters are arranged within those institutions in a way that ensures that many tasks are actually accomplished.

1. Responsibility for carrying out specified activities is delegated to individuals up and down the status hierarchy.

2. Authority to make the necessary decisions and implement the necessary tasks is delegated to those same individuals.

3. Information about policies and procedures is provided so that individuals can not only carry out routine tasks but also deal with unusual occurrences, identify problems, effect solutions, and make autonomous decisions within the scope of their responsibility.

Americans believe that responsibility, authority, and accurate information should be inextricably linked and at the disposal of individual employees. They believe that an individual should be in charge of any important activity, even within an institutional setting. Within his or her scope of responsibility and within the guidelines and policies set by leaders and supervisors, each employee is expected to take initiative, achieve goals, make things work efficiently, solve problems, and generally make progress for the company or institution.

Equally important, the employee should distinguish him- or herself as a person who is imaginative, energetic, competent, productive, and a decision maker—in colloquial terms, a "self-starter," a "doer," a "go-getter." Many jobs do not lend themselves perfectly to these individually oriented conditions and opportunities, but these are the ideals that people in the United States hold dear and that, in some cases, are actually attained in practice.

Ambitious employees in U.S. institutional settings have as their objective moving up the status hierarchy. Higher and higher levels bring greater wealth, increased prestige, and—most important for our purposes—broader powers enabling decisions to affect an ever widening sweep of people, material resources, procedures, and events. Although consultation with others regarding many decisions (especially large ones) is obligatory, most decisions, large or small, are traceable to a single individual. High-status individuals are those who make—and are accountable for—the big decisions. This is the meaning of power in the United States.

Institutional Decision-Making Values in the People's Republic

Anthropologists and sociologists have recognized for a long time that Chinese values accentuate the importance of the major primary groups to which each person belongs. The primary group is viewed as the basic unit of survival. Edwin C. Nevis, who has interpreted Chinese culture using "actualization" and other concepts popularized by Abraham H. Maslow, observes that the Chinese focus on actualization of the group while Americans stress actualization of the individual. American assumptions, says Nevis, reflect equality of opportunity; Chinese assumptions focus on equality in the sharing of output. To the extent that the Chinese can conceive of self-actualization, they would define it as the realization of personal potential in direct relation to the needs of the group (such as family, work unit, or nation). For example, they might offer, "To achieve China's four modernizations, I must...."[4] Within this context, harmony in interpersonal relationships is of paramount importance and calls for enormous sensitivity to the needs, priorities, feelings, and sense of dignity of other group members. Conformity to group norms is viewed positively; distinguishing oneself from other group members in any way that disrupts the smooth flow of human relationships is criticized.

Productive activities do occur in Chinese institutions. Workers cannot get away with being completely unproductive, but neither are they judged solely on the basis of their productivity.[5] And because of their heavy dependence upon those above them in the hierarchy, individual workers are not expected to try to improve aspects of the system, deal on their own initiative with unusual requests to the work unit, or make decisions about matters that they have not been assigned to handle.

Within Chinese institutions, individuals have responsibility for carrying out specified tasks just as in U.S. institutions. But the exceptionally high degree of dependence upon leaders that is typical in China carries with it the logic that the leader's authority is not delegated downward along with responsibility for carrying out specific routines. Subordinates are therefore unlikely to take authority upon themselves. This reluctance to assume authority is reinforced by the fact that, in general, accountability for decisions is evaded in a collectivist culture. If a decision for which an individual appears to be accountable is later determined to be wrong for any practical or political reason, that individual may be subjected to criticism or even punishment.[6]

Furthermore, Chinese lower-level functionaries possess relatively little detailed information about their leader's point of view. Like authority, information is not passed very far downward. Since they lack both information and authority, lower-level functionaries are usually discouraged from making decisions about any matter outside their routine responsibilities.[7]

How American Expectations Run Afoul of Chinese Realities

It should be reasonably clear why Americans become frustrated with Chinese decision-making practices. Americans bring to encounters with a Chinese institution an expectation that employees will be motivated, at least to some extent, to take personal initiative in dealing with whatever concerns are brought to their attention by people (such as Americans in China) who are served by the institution.

So long as an American's request is wholly within the jurisdiction of the Chinese functionary and is wholly covered by that functionary's routine responsibilities and procedures, chances are that action will be forthcoming within a more or less reasonable length of time. (What is considered a reasonable length of time to do something is, of course, subject to different cultural interpretations.) But when the American's request is out of the ordinary, the possibility arises that the Chinese functionary might have to exercise discretion, take individual initiative, and thereby run two risks: exceeding authority (which has not been delegated) and acting without full information about the policies and intentions of his or her superiors.

The outcome is that the American may not get what is desired or may get it only after an extended delay. Americans, accustomed to a comparatively high degree of efficiency in their dealings with organizations, are understandably upset. But for them to expect any other modus operandi is to expect what is nearly impossible.

Five Differences between Chinese and American Negotiating Practices

Types of Institutions Represented

Although Chinese negotiators are clearly identified with a certain institution such as a manufacturing complex, a university, or an import-export company, they ultimately represent the interests and viewpoints of the government, frequently the central government in Beijing. American negotiators almost always represent private firms. Even those representing state universities in the United States do not have the same kind of relationship to government that Chinese negotiators have. (An obvious exception is government-to-government negotiations by the U.S. diplomatic corps.)

As representatives of government, Chinese negotiators are keenly aware of national or regional pride, of the public interest as viewed by political authorities, and of the political ideology espoused by their governmental leaders. They are committed to maintaining political correctness at all times and rarely have the authority to make the final decision for the Chinese side regarding the proposals being debated at the negotiating table. Rather, they are obliged to seek approval at several levels up the administrative ladder for all agreements they tentatively make during the negotiations.

Most American negotiators would be astonished or insulted by the suggestion that their point of view was adopted in order to be politically correct. Generally, American negotiators are preoccupied with the profitability of their company or the prestige of their university. Some Americans must obtain final approval from a chief executive officer or board of directors for the agreements they reach abroad, but many come to China with complete authority to make final decisions.

Types of Relationships Envisioned

Chinese institutional representatives expect that negotiations will lead to a partnership characterized by trust, obligations of mutual support, and permanence. For them, negotiations are important social occasions, a basic purpose of which is to foster a relationship between the two sides that will take root, grow, and flower during the present and, more important, long into the future. They need to convince themselves of the suitability of their counterparts; and once those counterparts are deemed suitable, they want to nurture the kind of interpersonal sensitivity, harmony, mutual obligation, and durability that ideally characterizes all Chinese relationships.[8]

Americans are hardly averse to good social relationships but rarely see the building of a permanent partnership as one of their principal goals. As negotiators in many parts of the world have remarked, Americans are more inclined than any other national group of businesspeople to rush headlong into making a deal, seemingly with little concern about the level of trust established with their counterparts. Their overriding objective seems to be the signing of an advantageous contract, and the sooner the better.

Americans believe they are protected by the binding legal nature of the contract and therefore give little weight to the development of positive and enduring personal relationships. They tend to view each contract as a separate and distinct transaction, a "done deal," that obliges them to carry out specific tasks over a limited or defined period of time but does not oblige them to develop personal relationships or continue them beyond the period of the initial agreement unless they believe that it would be advantageous to do so.

Believing that business must be conducted on the basis of mutual trust, Chinese negotiators closely observe the comportment of their foreign counterparts at all times. In contrast, Americans tend to believe that their professionalism, seriousness of purpose, and general civility are under inspection only, or at least primarily, when they are at the bargaining table. At other times—on sightseeing tours organized by their Chinese hosts, for instance—they often lapse into a customary informality of dress and behavior that undermines their image of competent professionalism, especially if it goes to the extreme of backslapping ribaldry. The Chinese use every informal encounter to evaluate the temperament, sincerity, and seriousness of their potential trading partners.[9]

Basic Approaches to Negotiating

The Chinese are not nearly as legalistic as are Americans[10] and do not completely share the American view that a contract is a complete, binding, limiting set of specifications. Because the emphasis of the Chinese is more on the long-term possibilities inherent in the partnership and less on the specific transaction to be enshrined therein, their approach is to begin by discussing in broad terms the mutual interests that are shared, or could be shared, by the institutions involved. Their objective is typically to avoid discussing details in this early phase; instead, they want to reach an agreement on general principles governing the evolving relationship.

Americans distrust talk of general principles, regarding it as too philosophical or merely rhetorical. To Americans, progress in negotiations is made by getting down to work on the details. A good relationship is the product of agreement on many specific items, a process facilitated by each side's willingness and ability to appreciate the other's point of view, basic motives, and practical constraints.

Lucian Pye has drawn the following distinction between the two approaches. Americans tend to begin by enthusiastically promoting their best-case view of how the details could be worked out, then gradually pull back through a series of compromises to whatever arrangements appeal to the Chinese. The Chinese tend to begin with discussions of mutual interests and general principles. When they have the Americans committed to these—a commitment that the Americans may not take very seriously because of the absence of details—the Chinese try, through appeals to those mutual interests, to induce the Americans to agree to the Chinese view of what the details should be. To the Chinese way of thinking, the durable and trusting relationship established in the early phase of the negotiations should remove any precise limits on what one party should do for the other. Since the Americans clearly come from the more technologically advanced society, they should be ready and willing to help the Chinese in as many ways as possible.[11]

There may be much talk about *youyi*, or "friendship," during the early phase. What the Chinese mean by friendship in this context is not the largely sentimental feelings that Americans associate with friendship or the American notion that friends are those with whom one can be completely informal. To the Chinese, friends in a business or institutional relationship are people who recognize that the manner in which those involved interact and relate to each other is very important and involves due respect for rank and position. In business friendships, the Chinese expect the type of long-term trust, practical dependency, and mutual obligation that they associate with guanxi. This helps to explain why people who have been doing business in China for a few years are more likely to be favored by the Chinese when new business opportunities arise; they are trusted "old friends" with whom obligations have been built up.[12]

The Chinese view of the relationship developed during negotiations leads them to do something that perplexes, even infuriates, Americans. After the contract has been approved and signed by the principals on both sides, the Chinese often continue to bring up possible new arrangements and adjustments. From the American point of view, the transaction is complete; the task now is to carry out its terms. But the Chinese see the transaction as but an incident in a long-term relationship characterized by friendship, understanding, and mutual dependency and support. There should be no inhibitions regarding further discussions about what each party can do for the other in order to promote their shared interests.

Perspectives on the Nature of Contracts

Chinese negotiators usually arrive at the bargaining table either with no draft contract or with a rather simple one based on a standard pattern often used in China. American negotiators usually arrive with a long and complicated draft contract that is situation-specific and reflects the highly legalistic nature of business in the United States. It is not unusual for the Chinese to insist, without having read the Americans' draft, that it be shortened and simplified. This request is not only for their own benefit but also for the benefit of the higher-ranking officials who must approve their positions at the bargaining table but who may be less well prepared by education and experience to understand American legalistic circumlocutions.

The fundamental problem, though, is not the length and complexity of the document itself but rather differences in what each side sees as the nature and purpose of a contract. From the American point of view, a contract focuses in great detail on the specific rights and responsibilities of the two parties. A major purpose of a contract is to compel each side to do, within a limited and defined span of time, everything that it has promised to do. Another purpose is to deal in advance with the possibility of worst-case scenarios such as a breakdown in contractual relations.

The Chinese think that the principal purpose of a contract is to establish a positive relationship between the two parties, one that focuses generally on shared interests and will continue indefinitely. The notion that the two parties could come into serious conflict is not entertained. The idea that the two parties should write out in great detail what each will and will not do is not seen as necessary. The Chinese focus on positive overall outcomes. In their view, during the negotiating sessions the two sides are working in a spirit of mutual support toward drafting a written agreement regarding their cooperation in attaining broadly stated goals.

One unfortunate outcome of these differing views is that one side may attempt to educate the other about the proper way to carry out the negotiations. When this occurs, it is a source of irritation for the people on the other side, who see it as gratuitous instruction.[13]

Another unfortunate outcome of these differing views, at least from the legalistic American perspective, is that the Chinese do not always accept contracts as absolutely binding. If the policies of the Chinese government change significantly between the signing of a contract and the completion of its implementation, the Chinese may seek to renegotiate or decline to adhere to a strict interpretation of the terms of the existing contract.[14]

Amounts of Time Required to Complete the Process

Almost everyone who has been through negotiations in China complains about the delays that occur and stresses the patience needed by Americans and other Westerners. One reason for this slow pace is, as mentioned earlier, that Chinese negotiators have no authority to make final commitments. They must discuss all contract provisions with colleagues (some of whom may be present, some of whom may not) and must seek input from superiors on all major questions. Approval of the final agreement almost always needs to be sought from officials at several higher levels in the hierarchy.

Stanley B. Lubman, who has represented American business interests in China for more than a decade, notes that one result of this characteristic is that Chinese negotiators, unlike their American counterparts, are rarely free to alter their position to any extent during the actual face-to-face sessions.

> If they encounter opposition, Chinese negotiators tend to do no more than restate their original argument. It would be extraordinary for Chinese to change a major position without having discussed it among themselves first, which they will commonly do between negotiating sessions.
>
> By contrast, an American negotiator may change his position in mid-argument or engage in variations on the original one, and may often be flexible enough to consult with his colleagues in midsession.
>
> These differences probably stem from the bureaucratic nature of the Chinese organizations involved. The Chinese negotiator's position has most likely been arrived at by a group, approved by his superiors within his own organization and perhaps also cleared with other organizations; as a result, his authority to vary from that position without prior consultation is extremely limited.[15]

A second reason for the slow pace of negotiations is that the two sides have differing views about the ultimate purpose of the document they are attempting to fashion and therefore about precisely what they ought to be discussing. Being at cross-purposes, they require more time jointly to work things out than if they were in negotiations with counterparts who shared most or all of their basic assumptions.

A final reason for the extended duration of most negotiations is, as noted earlier, that the Chinese want to develop a partnership with a feeling of mutual trust and an aura of permanence. The entire process has social value for the Chinese. They view the actual bargaining sessions and the time in between (when approvals are being sought) with a much lower sense of urgency than do most American negotiators.

People who have observed and commented upon negotiations between Chinese and American counterparts have cautioned that the tendency of Americans to be in a rush annoys some Chinese[16] and can place the Americans in an unfavorable position commercially.

A Note about American Women Working in China

Some American companies express concern about sending their female professionals to Asia as expatriates. They fear that the women might not be respected by local men and that, as a result, the women might not be able to attain their business objectives.

With respect to the PRC, evidence is accumulating that female American expats are usually just as effective as American males and are often *more* effective in attaining their objectives...and without suffering any sort of discrimination. In fact, American women working in China and Chinese women with experience working in the United States comment that women feel more accepted as professionals in China than in the United States.

Why is this the case? In the United States, the prevailing expectation is that adult women will have a choice between being gainfully employed and being a homemaker. When women have young children, this presumption of choice puts them on the horns of a dilemma: if they stay at home, they risk low peer respect because they are not "working." If they work, they risk societal prejudice because their children lack a full-time mother. Also, all women, married or single, risk being categorized by some male coworkers primarily on the basis of their gender rather than their experience, intelligence, productivity, and/or seniority.

In the PRC, the prevailing expectation about adult women has always been that they will be gainfully employed. The result is that many senior positions in business, science, and other fields are held by women. But what about their children? Here, perhaps, is the critical difference. In China, children are taken care of by *all* adults in their extended family—most of whom either live under the same roof or within walking or bicycling distance—or by child-care centers in their danwei. Therefore, not only do Chinese women avoid the Americans' dilemma, but they are also accepted as full and equal partners with men on the job.

Finally, two personal leadership qualities are valued by the Chinese. One is competence. The other is *ren*, which means "warmheartedness, benevolence, and readiness to care for others." The Confucian basis for this thinking is that if a leader is ren and takes good care of subordinates, he or she will receive their loyalty in turn. Adopting ren behavior is more common among American women than among American men. Thus, U.S. companies need not hesitate to send competent female professionals to China.[17]

---

[1] During the 1950s, 1960s, and 1970s, the People's Republic was governed according to a model in which municipal and provincial leaders of government were under the control of the central government just as were leaders in every other walk of life. Ministries were involved in policy making and in commercial and industrial management. Now, most ministry officials are not allowed to discharge both sets of responsibilities. The commercial and industrial operations of many ministries have been turned into separate enterprises; for example, the Chinese Light Industrial and Technology Corporation was formerly the commercial arm of the Ministry of Light Industry.

[2] In order to find out what features of Chinese communicative and social behavior were proving the most perplexing or troublesome for Americans living and working in China, the two authors surveyed some twenty Americans, most of whom were employed in Beijing during 1986. (Several extended interviews were also carried out.) The respondents were found to object most strongly to two behaviors of the Chinese: their frequent heavy smoking and their decision-making practices. Several respondents expressed intense frustration over what they perceived as the virtual inability of Chinese cadres and minor officials to

make any decisions, even regarding trivial matters, in a timely manner.

3 For a thought-provoking description and analysis by two Americans about how they ran afoul of Chinese decision-making procedures, see Cindy P. Lindsay and Bobby L. Dempsey, "Ten Painfully Learned Lessons about Working in China: The Insights of Two American Behavioral Scientists," *Journal of Applied Behavioral Science* 19, no. 3 (1983).

4 Edwin C. Nevis, "Using an American Perspective in Understanding Another Culture: Toward a Hierarchy of Needs for the People's Republic of China," *Journal of Applied Behavioral Science* 19, no. 3 (1983): 254, 261–62. Self-actualization is a concept that originated within an individualistic value system; the Chinese are not likely to use this term as we are using it here.

5 Another factor that may prevent Chinese workers from striving to be efficient and productive is the "iron rice bowl" concept that, in effect, ensures that every worker will be paid regardless of the quantity and quality of work performed. The Chinese government has been trying to do away with the iron rice bowl. In the past few years, malfunctioning state enterprises have been allowed to go bankrupt or be merged with larger, efficient, profit-making enterprises. As a consequence, large numbers of workers have been laid off, invalidating the iron rice bowl concept, at least for these workers. Note also that foreign-owned and joint-venture enterprises have the right to hire and fire their employees; the iron rice bowl does not apply to them at all.

6 Retribution for previous errors, or what were claimed to be errors, was dealt out freely during the Cultural Revolution, even in cases in which the decision, action, or opinion in question was perfectly reasonable at the time it occurred. Among the Chinese there is a lingering fear that what happened during the Cultural Revolution could happen again.

7 Redding and Wong write that Chinese vertical relationships within institutional contexts can be summarized as follows:
    a. The individual has an unavoidable responsibility for his or her own actions.
    b. The top-down tradition of authority leaves little room for subordinate initiative.

c. Subordinate behavior which is not in tune with the leader's intentions is likely to have serious repercussions for the subordinate.

d. Goals will normally be derived from the leader's intentions and may not be openly and clearly defined.

e. A test of loyalty is the capacity [of the subordinate] to understand and espouse these intentions.

Gordon Redding and Gilbert Y. Y. Wong, "The Psychology of Chinese Organizational Behaviour," in *The Psychology of the Chinese People*, edited by Michael Harris Bond (Hong Kong: Oxford University Press, 1986), 288–89.

[8] Jonathan M. Zamet and Murray E. Bovarnick, reporting the findings of extensive research carried out among expatriates and Chinese officials by Organizational Resources Counselors, Inc., say that the key to business relationships in China is the building up of trust and mutual respect. This requires as much as six months, during which the Chinese carefully watch every aspect of their counterparts' behavior. Jonathan M. Zamet and Murray E. Bovarnick, "Employee Relations for Multinational Companies in China," *Columbia Journal of World Business* 21, no. 1 (Spring 1986): 14.

Lucian W. Pye has summarized the difference between the Chinese and American views of the intended relationship as follows:

The American goal is a binding agreement secured by a stable and enduring legal system, a contract with all the power and mystique we associate with the law. The Chinese see stability not in the power of the law but in the strength of human relationships. A contract establishes what is essentially a personal relationship. Although the Chinese are now developing a more institutionalized legal system, their culture still reflects a philosophy that governance is more by people than by laws.

Lucian W. Pye, "The China Trade: Making the Deal," *Harvard Business Review* 64, no. 4 (July-August 1986): 79.

[9] Arne J. de Keijzer, *The China Business Handbook* (Weston, CT: Asia Business Communications, 1986), 127, 129.

[10] For a short but instructive comparison of the Chinese and American approach to legal matters, see Victor H. Li, *Law without Lawyers: A Comparative View of Law in China and the United States* (Boulder, CO: Westview Press, 1978).

[11] Lucian W. Pye, *Chinese Commercial Negotiating Style* (Cambridge, MA: Oelgeschlager, Gunn & Hain, 1982), 77, 89.

[12] de Keijzer, *The China Business Handbook*, 124, 138. Oded Shenkar and Simcha Ronen, "The Cultural Context of Negotiations: The Implications of Chinese Interpersonal Norms," *Journal of Applied Behavioral Science* 23, no. 2 (1987): 271.

[13] Stanley B. Lubman, "Negotiations in China: Observations of a Lawyer," in *Communicating with China*, edited by Robert A. Kapp (Yarmouth, ME: Intercultural Press, 1983), 64–65, 67–68.

[14] Lindsay and Dempsey, "Ten Painfully Learned Lessons about Working in China," 267.

[15] Lubman, "Negotiations in China," 66–67.

[16] "The West tends to reward Type A personalities. In China they are shunned as misfits, both socially and professionally," de Keijzer, *The China Business Handbook*, 135.

[17] The authors are indebted to Kay M. Jones for these insights.

Additional Readings on Commercial Practices among the Chinese

Items preceded by an asterisk are annotated in "Recommended Readings."

For a broad overview of the kinds of difficulties faced by Western companies and their expatriate representatives (and accompanying family members) in the People's Republic, consult the following.

Victor H. Li. *Law without Lawyers: A Comparative View of Law in China and the United States*. Boulder, CO: Westview Press, 1978.

Lipper, Hal. "Employers Maneuver to Help Expats Survive in China." *Asian Wall Street Journal*, 16 September 1997, 13.

Renwick, George. "China's Real Challenge to Expats." *International Insight* (published by Runzheimer International), (Summer 1996): 4–6.

Tung, Rosalie L. "Corporate Executives and Their Families in China: The Need for Cross-Cultural Understanding in Business." *Columbia Journal of World Business* 21, no. 1 (Spring 1986): 21–25.

Zamet, Jonathan M., and Murray E. Bovarnick. "Employee Relations for Multinational Companies in China." *Columbia Journal of World Business* 21, no. 1 (Spring 1986): 13–19.

For general advice and guidelines about doing business in the People's Republic in a culturally sensitive manner, consult the following.

*de Keijzer, Arne J. *China: Business Strategies for the '90s.* Berkeley, CA: Pacific View Press, 1992.

*Jones, Stephanie. *Managing in China: An Executive Survival Guide.* Singapore: Butterworth-Heinemann Asia, 1997.

*Macleod, Roderick. *China, Inc.: How to Do Business with the Chinese.* New York: Bantam Books, 1988.

*Seligman, Scott D. *Dealing with the Chinese: A Practical Guide to Business Etiquette in the People's Republic Today.* New York: Warner Books, 1989. Rev. ed. forthcoming 1999.

*Yang, Mayfair Mei-hui. *Gifts, Favors and Banquets: The Art of Social Relationships in China.* Ithaca: Cornell University Press, 1994.

For analyses of the Chinese negotiating style and how it differs from the American style, consult the following.

Lubman, Stanley B. "Negotiations in China: Observations of a Lawyer." In *Communicating with China,* edited by Robert A. Kapp. Yarmouth, ME: Intercultural Press, 1983.

Shenkar, Oded, and Simcha Ronen. "The Cultural Context of Negotiations: The Implications of Chinese Interpersonal Norms." *Journal of Applied Behavioral Science* 23, no. 2 (1987): 263–75.

*Pye, Lucian W. *Chinese Negotiating Style: Commercial Approaches and Cultural Principles*. Rev. ed. New York: Quorum Books, 1992.

————. "The China Trade: Making the Deal." *Harvard Business Review* 64, no. 4 (July-August 1986): 74, 76–80.

Randt, Clark T. "Negotiating Strategy and Tactics." In *U.S.-China Trade: Problems and Prospects*, edited by Eugene K. Lawson. New York: Praeger, 1988.

*Seligman, Scott D. *Dealing with the Chinese: A Practical Guide to Business Etiquette in the People's Republic Today*. New York: Warner Books, 1989. Rev. ed. forthcoming 1999.

For perspectives on Chinese psychology and behavior in political and organizational contexts, consult the following.

*Bond, Michael Harris. "Chinese Organizational Life." In *Beyond the Chinese Face: Insights from Psychology*. Hong Kong: Oxford University Press, 1991. See chapter 6, "Chinese Organizational Life."

*Bond, Michael Harris, and Kwang-kuo Hwang. "The Social Psychology of the Chinese People." In *The Psychology of the Chinese People*, edited by Michael Harris Bond. Hong Kong: Oxford University Press, 1986. See especially the subsections that deal with leadership, conformity, and aggression and conflict.

Greenblatt, Sidney L. et al. *Organizational Behavior in Chinese Society*. New York: Praeger, 1981.

Hendryx, Steven R. "The China Trade: Making the Deal Work." *Harvard Business Review* 64, no. 4 (July-August 1986): 75, 81–84.

Nevis, Edwin C. "Using an American Perspective in Understanding Another Culture: Toward a Hierarchy of Needs for the People's Republic of China." *Journal of Applied Behavioral Science* 19, no. 3 (1983): 249–64.

Pye, Lucian W. *Asian Power and Politics: The Cultural Dimensions of Authority*. Cambridge, MA: The Belknap Press, 1985. See especially chapters 1, 3, 7, and 11.

Redding, Gordon, and Gilbert Y. Y. Wong. "The Psychology of Chinese Organizational Behaviour." In *The Psychology of the Chinese People*, edited by Michael Harris Bond. Hong Kong:

Oxford University Press, 1986. See especially the subsections that deal with leadership and decision making, management control, and social stability.

Smith, Peter B., and Zhong-Ming Wang. "Chinese Leadership and Organizational Structure." In *The Handbook of Chinese Psychology*, edited by Michael Harris Bond. Hong Kong: Oxford University Press, 1996.

For thought-provoking stories about the interactions of American and Chinese officials during negotiations or in other organizational contexts, consult the following.

Browning, Graeme. *If Everybody Bought One Shoe: American Capitalism in Communist China.* New York: Hill & Wang, 1989.

*Holm, Bill. *Coming Home Crazy: An Alphabet of China Essays.* Minneapolis: Milkweed Editions, 1990.

Lindsay, Cindy P., and Bobby L. Dempsey. "Ten Painfully Learned Lessons about Working in China: The Insights of Two American Behavioral Scientists." *Journal of Applied Behavioral Science* 19, no. 3 (1983): 265–76.

Mann, Jim. *Beijing Jeep: The Short, Unhappy Romance of American Business in China.* New York: Simon & Schuster, 1989.

For discussions of cross-cultural communication problems affecting American affairs in East Asia, and of remedies for those problems, consult the following.

James, David L. *The Executive Guide to Asia-Pacific Communications: Doing Business across the Pacific.* Tokyo and New York: Kodansha, 1995.

Thomson, James C., Peter W. Stanley, and John Curtis Perry. *Sentimental Imperialists: The American Experience in East Asia.* New York: Harper Colophon Books, 1981.

For additional annotated bibliographies regarding business relations and negotiations in the PRC, consult the following.

de Keijzer, Arne J. *The China Business Handbook.* Weston, CT: Asia Business Communications, 1986. This bibliography has a broad focus; de Keijzer's annotations are short.

116

*Macleod, Roderick. *China, Inc.: How to Do Business with the Chinese*. New York: Bantam Books, 1988. This bibliography focuses on the cultural barriers to China-U.S. negotiations; Macleod's annotations are lengthy and helpful.

An excellent way to keep up with the latest business-related events in the PRC and the rest of Asia, and with recently published books related to business in the region, is to subscribe to the weekly *Far Eastern Economic Review*, published in Hong Kong. For more information, contact the Review Publishing Company, GPO Box 160, Hong Kong; telephone: 011-852-2508-4338; fax: 011-852-2503-1549; Website: http://www.feer.com

10

十

The Concept of "Face" in Chinese-American Interaction*

A General Explanation of the Concept of Face

Americans rarely speak about face, so you might suspect that concern for face is a Chinese (or Asian) preoccupation. But sociologists know that the concept exists among Americans as well as among the Chinese.[1] Scholars who have examined the face concept have pronounced it a universal concern of human beings.[2]

In all societies, each person (not including infants and small children or those suffering from serious mental illness) presents him- or herself as a certain type of human being to relatives, friends, colleagues, acquaintances, and even to

---

* We have relied heavily in the preparation of this chapter on the work of Michael Harris Bond and two of his collaborators: (1) Bond and Peter W. H. Lee, "Face Saving in Chinese Culture: A Discussion and Experimental Study of Hong Kong Students," and (2) Bond and Kwang-kuo Hwang, "The Social Psychology of the Chinese People," both in *Social Life and Development in Hong Kong*, edited by Ambrose Y. C. King and Rance P. L. Lee. 213–66.

strangers. This means that the person claims to be someone with certain characteristics and traits. One generally makes such claims by implicit means: dialect and accent, topics of discussion, attire and self-decoration, usual patterns of behavior, values and attitudes (inferred from behaviors), choice of companions, and so on. One might also make such claims by explicit (verbal) means: "I am such-and-such a type of person. I usually do thus-and-so when faced with a certain kind of situation."[3]

Human characteristics and traits can vary enormously. Here are just six examples drawn from the dozens of parameters along which human differences can be described. Each is deliberately stated in terms of polar opposites, whereas, of course, any given human being can be described as existing anywhere on the continuum between those two opposites: (1) concern or lack of concern for attractive physical appearance; (2) preference for order or disorder in maintaining one's possessions; (3) concern or lack of concern for religious values and practices; (4) preference for self-restraint or self-indulgence; (5) tendency to be nurturing and kind, or stern and demanding, toward others; and (6) tendency to be creative or conformist in thinking.

As people grow into adulthood, they gradually adopt certain claims regarding their own characteristics and traits, and they learn to make these claims, implicitly and sometimes explicitly, to others. People also learn to recognize other individuals' implicit claims about themselves and to accept (or in some cases to appear to accept) those claims. One might say that people learn to accept "at face value" another person's "line" regarding the type of person that he or she is. This set of claims, or line, of each person is his or her face.

In every social situation, everyone present is putting forward a certain face. As long as each person accepts every other person's face, the social situation can proceed relatively smoothly in the sense that personal relationships can develop and business can be transacted. Mutual acceptance of another's face does not guarantee that people will agree about everything or will feel highly positive about one another. Personal relationships may develop toward friendship or enmity; business dealings may yield deals or disappointment. The point is that the focus of the social situation is the desires and concerns of its participants, not the implicit claims of those participants about their traits and characteristics.

It is entirely possible to call into question the claims of any person regarding his or her characteristics and traits. One may do this in an explicit manner, as occurs when someone cries out in anger to another, "You are a liar! You are a fraud!" In such a case, the focus of the social situation shifts abruptly from the desires and concerns of its participants to the image that one of the participants has been putting forward to the others. To be accused of lying or fraud is to have one's face called into question, to have one's apparent integrity impugned. The accusers are saying, in effect, "Your traits and characteristics are not what you want us to believe they are." For the accused, this is a most difficult and embarrassing moment, regardless of whether he or she is honest or deceitful.

It is also possible to call into question a person's face in an implicit manner. Doing so requires that one fail to accept at face value the traits and characteristics the other person is claiming. There are countless ways of doing this; here are two examples.

1. Suppose that a new graduate student, proud of her straight-A college record, behaving as a young adult professional should and wearing her dress-for-success suit, enters the office of her new academic adviser. In the course of their conversation, he refers to her as a "girl," talks down to her by explaining a simple point in her field, and questions her ability to complete the academic year successfully. The adviser has implicitly called into question the young woman's claims about herself, causing her to lose face.

2. Suppose that, during a school holiday, a father takes his ten-year-old daughter with him to his office. The father's supervisor appears and, in full view of the daughter, severely criticizes the father for some error. In this case, the father's claims about himself to his supervisor are damaged; his claims about himself to his daughter are even more damaged. It is a supervisor's place to correct the errors of subordinates (though there are tactful as well as harsh ways of doing this). But the father feels deeply embarrassed in front of his daughter, since the validity of his face is likely to have been severely undermined from her point of view.

If you have ever told a white lie, you have a basis in your own experience for understanding face. The purpose of a white lie is to enable you to avoid calling into question the views that someone holds of him- or herself. It is, in other words, a face-saving device. The face that the white liar is saving may be his own as well as that of the person to whom the lie is told.

Purposeful duplicity is hardly the only way to maintain one's own face and that of acquaintances. Personal qualities such as tact, diplomacy, and sensitivity, which are admired by Americans, are related to one's ability to recognize and preserve others' claims for themselves. So, even though people in the United States rarely talk about face, they do recognize its existence as well as its value in enabling all parties to a social interaction to maintain their claims.

The basic parameters of the face concept, then, are these.
1. Each person's set of personal claims is socially vital as a pattern of characteristics that other people can recognize and expect to be more or less consistent. Others learn to interact with that person in order to transact business or develop a relationship.
2. Each person's set of personal claims is psychologically vital as the pattern of characteristics that constitutes his or her identity, generating a personal sense of dignity, integrity, and self-respect.

3. This set of claims about oneself is one's face, the sense of self that one puts forward to others with reasonable (if not perfect) consistency.

4. In any type of social situation, everyone present has a stake in preserving everyone else's face as well as his or her own; the mutual preservation of face enables social life to proceed. Tact, diplomacy, and sensitivity are among the admirable behavioral qualities that enable the parties to a social interaction to do this successfully. White lying, perhaps less admirable, also enables people to preserve face.

5. Loss of face occurs when a person's set of claims is implicitly or explicitly called into question by others. Loss of face creates embarrassment and perhaps anger in the person so questioned because, with or without justification, it threatens to unmask the individual, to strip away the role he or she has been taking with others.

6. The person who has unintentionally caused another's loss of face is also likely to lose face because he or she probably views him- or herself as someone who is sufficiently tactful to avoid causing such embarrassment.

7. When anyone obviously loses face, the focus of the social situation quickly shifts, at least momentarily, to concern over what will be done about the situation by the person who lost face and by the person who caused the problem.

Contrasts between Chinese and American Concepts of Face

The difference in Chinese and American concepts of face is that face simply has greater social significance for the Chinese. In the United States, concern for face exists but remains largely out of most people's awareness. In the People's Republic, everyone is conscious of face all the time. An oft repeated Chinese proverb puts it thus: "A person needs face as a tree needs bark."

Why should concern for face have such high importance for the Chinese? There are two principal reasons. First, Chinese society over the centuries has typically been one of very restricted geographical mobility. People have had little opportunity to move away from the locality of their birth and each tends to spend his or her entire life in the company of the same friends, neighbors, and relatives. When one is attached for life to a given group of people, maintaining harmonious relationships among all its members becomes of paramount importance. Consequently, face-saving behaviors take on great significance; they maintain harmony, avoid conflicts, and protect the integrity of the group.[4]

Life in the United States has been mobile virtually from the earliest days of European colonization; colonial peoples did not hesitate to move on if life in a certain locality did not suit them. Thus, the composition of one's community and friendship groups changed often during one's lifetime; even relatives would be left behind when one decided to search elsewhere for a better life. Given the constant shifting of group membership, attention increasingly focused on individuals instead of on groups or collectives. As a result, the maintenance of group integrity and harmony rarely attained the significance for Americans that it customarily did for the Chinese.

Second, Confucius emphasized that humans exist in interactive relationships with others and that most human relationships are unequal in nature. Confucius found no fault with inequality because, in his view, the obligations between senior and junior ran in both directions. The senior party was assumed to have prerogatives and authority with respect to the junior party; but the senior party was also constrained in dealings with his or her junior by a morality of compassion and righteousness. The junior party, in turn, was bound to be respectful and obedient toward the senior party, but he or she also could confidently expect protection, loyalty, and mentorship from his or her senior.

These reciprocal obligations were expressed in the Chinese virtue known as *li*, which means "right conduct in maintaining one's place in the hierarchical order."[5] *Li* is now used by the average Chinese to mean decorum. Social harmony is preserved when all parties in a social situation behave in a decorous manner. One important way to be decorous is to accept and respect each person's need to maintain his or her face. Causing someone to lose face may well be construed as a challenge to his or her position in the hierarchy. Criticism of another person, especially of a superior, is fraught with danger. Loss of face is not merely a matter of personal embarrassment; it also threatens to disrupt the integrity of the group.

Although life in the United States certainly involves people in hierarchies, Americans typically make efforts to deemphasize the social distance implied in any superior-subordinate relationship and thus promote, at least superficially, an ethic of egalitarianism. Americans know the identities of those above and below them on the social-status scale, and they defer to those above them when necessary or expedient. But, in the main, they rely on their all-encompassing habit of informality to blur the distinctions of status and authority, to pretend, as it were, that all people are fundamentally the same. In addition, high social mobility has long characterized life in the United States and is widely thought to be a good thing. In a social context where there is relatively low authoritarianism and little preoccupation with maintaining a specific hierarchical order, loss of face causes personal embarrassment but does not necessarily threaten group integrity or unravel the fabric of social life.

If there is a qualitative difference between face in the two cultures, it may be related to the notion of integrity (wholeness, lack of internal contradictions). In the United States, individual integrity is uniquely important. In China, individual and group integrity are both important. In China, face can be lost as a result of undermining the long-established relationships that give a group its identity and its members a sense of security.[6]

Recognizing Common Face-Saving
Behaviors of the Chinese

Americans are hindered in dealing effectively with face-saving behaviors because they value directness in most ordinary social situations. They prefer to state matters (as they understand them) in a straightforward and accurate manner. Americans say no when their self-interest dictates that a negative reply is the necessary response. Americans say "I don't know" when, in fact, they don't know. They say "I can't do that" when what is requested is not in their power to grant. They occasionally tell white lies, but, more often, they tell it like it is even when they know that a straightforward, truthful response will not be emotionally pleasing to the other person.

Americans assume that each person is better able to advance his or her self-interest when the situation at hand is thoroughly understood by means of direct verbal communication. It's not that Americans don't value politeness and sensitivity. They do. They usually recognize when other people's feelings are at stake. But because they value directness more highly, they view their task in sensitive situations as giving complete information in a direct, if gentle, way.

Americans tend to assume that everyone else in the world is equally committed to directness in interpersonal communications. This assumption is erroneous, especially where the Chinese are concerned. The Chinese may very well on occasion be direct but only if no one, including themselves, will lose face. Consider three situations:

1. An American businesswoman is negotiating with a Chinese counterpart over an import agreement. She does not realize that one of her objectives cannot be accepted by the Chinese. When this objective comes up for discussion, the Chinese negotiator says that the American's request must receive further study. The American offers to further clarify the matter and asks about his objections. He mentions certain problems. After listening to

her clarifications, he responds, *Kaolü, kaolü,* which means "We'll think this over again" or "We must give it more thought." Why? Because stating his position directly would be to deny her request. This would damage his face by contradicting his implicit claim to be a person who lives in harmony with others. And it would damage her face by contradicting her implicit claim to be a negotiator who makes requests that are well informed and reasonable. The American feels frustrated. If she later learns that the Chinese simply could not agree to her request, she will think, "If only he had said no and had explained to me why it was impossible, I would have tried to figure out another way of making this deal attractive to my company." But her Chinese counterpart was concerned about his face and her face; he believed that avoiding loss of face was more important than making a deal in that round of negotiations.

2. A woman in China has a bad cold. An American acquaintance notices that she is uncomfortable and enthusiastically recommends his favorite remedy, long soaks in a tub of hot water. She thanks him, saying nothing about the fact that she has no tub and no access to anyone else's tub. Time passes and the Chinese woman's health improves. The American encounters her, notes that her cold is gone, and asks if she took his advice. She replies, "Oh, yes, it was wonderful." Another American happens to be present on this occasion; he knows that the woman could not have taken the advice. He later asks her why she claimed to enjoy the soaks. The Chinese woman replies, "I didn't want him to feel bad because I don't have a tub." Upon further questioning, she also admits that she had been reluctant to admit that she does not own a tub. So her little white lie saved her own face as well as that of the American tub enthusiast.

3. An American teacher in China has filled out an official form of some kind and has submitted it to the authorities

at his university. A Chinese clerk loses the form. Time goes by. The American, being efficiency-minded, soon becomes impatient. He asks the authorities who are dealing with the matter when action will be taken. He is told that the matter has been referred to a higher bureau for a decision, or perhaps that the matter is under review, or whatever. He is not told that the form has been lost. Why? Because losing a form is a type of incompetence, the exposure of which would cause the authorities to lose face by contradicting their implicit claim to be people who can properly handle forms. The American eventually suspects that the explanation being offered is not accurate. If he discovers that the form has actually been lost, he will feel angry because "After all, if I had only been told it was lost, I could have filled out another form and eliminated this interminable delay." But the authorities were more concerned about preserving face than about the efficient processing of forms or directness in communications.

In your encounters with the face-saving behaviors of your Chinese acquaintances, you may be tempted on rare occasions to accuse them of deliberately lying. Such an accusation may vent your frustration but otherwise is contrary to your own best interests, for the type of lie that injures others— what might be called a "black lie"—is as ethically wrong in China as it is in the United States. If you accuse a Chinese person of lying, you will cause him or her to lose face in a serious way. Therefore, you will also suffer a grievous loss of face, one from which it may be quite difficult to recover.

Protecting Your Own Face (and That of Others) When among the Chinese

The Chinese do not bring face considerations into every situation. Face considerations come into play most often when there is unpleasant news to be broken or when a difficult matter must be dealt with. You should be alert regarding face when interacting with the Chinese, but you certainly need not live in constant fear that you may offend someone with a casual remark.

Good advice about how to avoid experiencing or causing a loss of face comes from the scholar Kuo-shu Yang. Yang says that the Chinese, in deciding upon their own behavior, attach great weight to the anticipated reactions of others.

> Basically, [a Chinese acts] in accordance with external expectations or social norms, rather than internal wishes or personal integrity, so that he would be able to protect his [or her] social self and function as an integral part of the social network.

The behavioral consequences of this determination to function as an integral part of the social network include

> a predisposition toward such behavior patterns as social conformity, nonoffensive strategy, submission to social expectations, and worry about external opinions in an attempt to achieve [one's purposes].[7]

The two behaviors Yang describes as typically Chinese—ignoring internal wishes and the dictates of personal integrity and submitting to others' opinions and social expectations—run counter to the grain of most Americans. Even when Americans try to be nonaggressive and flexible, they are likely to be interacting with others according to the basic American assumption that each individual is responsible for him- or herself and has certain "inalienable rights" vis-à-vis others. Thus, what seems flexible and nonaggressive to an American may be perceived as selfish and overly assertive to a harmony-loving Chinese. Such is the essence of cross-cultural misunderstandings.

Here are guidelines to assist you in deciding how to behave in a fairly wide range of situations when among Chinese acquaintances:

1. Be deferential to those above you by virtue of age or position.
2. Be considerate of those below you by virtue of age or position.
3. Do not expect that a Chinese will act contrary to group norms.
4. Do not insist that your hosts respect your rights or opinions.
5. Do not in any way defy your hosts' accepted moral standards.
6. Do not show anger; avoid confrontations.
7. If you must say no, try to do so as tactfully as possible.
8. If you must criticize, do so in private or, when in public, in the context of upgrading an entire working group's performance.

With respect to guideline eight above, we recommend that any public airing of criticism (even constructive criticism) or feedback be in the context of pointing out the strengths and weaknesses of the working group as a unit, without singling out any individual (directly or by implication) for blame or for praise. Encourage stronger members to help weaker members improve; encourage weaker members to learn from stronger ones. This approach addresses your principal objective—upgrading performance—as well as your Chinese coworkers' principal objective—strengthening harmonious intragroup relationships.

Dealing with a Face-Loss Situation You Have Caused

If you become aware that a Chinese friend or colleague's behavior toward you has undergone a noticeably negative change, or that it is much more difficult to obtain assistance or information from a Chinese person on whom you relied in the past, one possible explanation is that you have caused him or her to lose face.

If you find that you have done just that, treat the situation seriously, for in causing the loss, you have also lost face. If you are still doing whatever it was that caused the loss of face, stop immediately. If you are not sure what the appropriate new behavior should be, try to find out from a trusted Chinese colleague or an expatriate with long experience in China. If you and the person you offended are on good terms with a mutual acquaintance (preferably a Chinese), ask the acquaintance to mediate.

Whether or not you make initial use of an intermediary, you should eventually approach the person you have offended in complete privacy. Apologize for your mistake and ask forgiveness. Explain your ideas about changing your behavior, and ask for advice regarding whether that change will enable you in the future to avoid causing that person and others loss of face.[8]

Assuming that you are able to resolve the matter in this way, be especially respectful and considerate of that person in the future. Help to restore the person's face by showing every regard for his or her status, needs, and implicit claims.

The Chinese sometimes deal with relatively minor face-loss situations by pretending that the offensive situation never occurred. If you find that your error is being treated in this manner, you certainly have the option of going along with the pretense. Nevertheless, you might try to improve the relationship gradually by showing special regard for the person in the future.

---

[1] The eminent American sociologist Erving Goffman has written as follows about face in an American context.

> [Face is] the positive social value a person effectively claims for himself by the line others assume he has taken during a particular contact. Face is an image of self delineated in terms of approved social attributes.

Erving Goffman, "On Face-Work," *Psychiatry* 18 (1955): 213.

2 See, for example, D. Y. F. Ho, "On the Concept of Face," *American Journal of Sociology* 81 (1976): 867–84.

3 We are leaving aside the question of how a person comes to make such claims. For example, is one existentially free to become as one wills, or are one's claims largely predetermined? If predetermined, is heredity or environment more responsible?

4 One's associations with others are critical to a Chinese person's self-image, so key relationships receive intense attention and commitment. Consequently, the difference between relationships with ingroup members and merely casual relationships is magnified. It may seem to Americans that the Chinese depersonalize strangers and casual acquaintances, ignoring their welfare in a callous manner. But the Chinese are simply focusing almost all of their energy on close relatives and intimate friends, in contrast to Americans, who put at least some effort into treating everyone, or almost everyone, more or less equally. (In sociological terms, particularism is characteristic of the Chinese while universalism is characteristic of Americans.) Someone once wondered how Confucius might view Christ's suggestion that one should do good to one's enemies. Confucius would say, "But if I do good to my enemies, what will I have left for my friends?"

5 L. E. Stover, *The Cultural Ecology of Chinese Civilization* (New York: New American Library, 1974). See chapter 16. Li originally referred to a set of rites and rituals associated with propriety in hierarchical relationships. *The Book of Rites*, thought to have been written by Confucius himself, describes these rituals. A Chinese saying dating from the time of Confucius that expresses the fixed hierarchical nature of proper relationships is "Seniors and juniors have their ranking."

6 In individualist cultures such as that of the United States, maintaining consistency between one's public and private self-images is of great importance; consequently, one's public self-presentation of face corresponds as closely as possible to one's "core self." But in collectivist cultures such as that of the PRC, the self is situationally and relationally based, defined by means of one's ongoing interpersonal relationships and maintained through reciprocal "facework negotiation" in which one is as committed

to lending role support to the face of others as to preserving one's own face. For a thorough discussion of these and related topics as well as a lengthy bibliography, see Stella Ting-Toomey, "Intercultural Conflict Styles: A Face-Negotiation Theory," in *Theories in Intercultural Communication. International and Intercultural Communication Annual* vol. 13, edited by Young Yun Kim and William B. Gudykunst (Newbury Park, CA: Sage, 1988), 213–35.

[7] Kuo-shu Yang, "Social Orientation and Individual Modernity among Chinese Students in Taiwan," *Journal of Social Psychology* 113 (1981): 159–60.

[8] Another possible approach, to be used only if the facts of the case dictate that it is more appropriate, is to address the person you have offended in complete privacy. Explain that the situation was one in which, for whatever reason, you were unable to act freely and could not avoid giving offense. Ask for understanding and pardon.

Part II:
Advice for Americans
Living and Working in the PRC

In this second part, we offer information and advice specifically for Americans who are, or soon will be, living and
working or studying in the People's Republic of China.

Living As a Foreign Guest
in the People's Republic

Preferential Treatment of Foreigners

Foreigners who have come to the PRC during recent decades in order to work with or assist the Chinese have been given preferential treatment. They have been housed in quarters that were often far more modern than those of any Chinese people around them, given perquisites in excess of those available to all but top local officials, fed with the highest-quality food that could be obtained, and paid salaries much higher than those of Chinese colleagues doing comparable work. They have been protected from some of the harsher realities of modern China and have been the recipients of enormous courtesy and care.

The original motivation for all this special attention came from at least three sources. First, as a poverty-stricken nation in economic and technical terms, China needed to attract and retain foreign experts who would assist in the modernization process. Second, many Chinese believed that people

136

from developed nations were so accustomed to modern comforts and conveniences that they would not be able to function competently without them. Finally, there was simple pride.

Now, with foreign professionals, educators, businesspeople, and others entering China in increasingly greater numbers since the opening of the country and acceleration of economic reforms, it is becoming impractical for the Chinese to deal with their "foreign friends" so carefully. But this change, like so many others, is occurring unevenly. Foreigners going to China today cannot accurately predict how they will be treated, though the probability is that their treatment will be more or less preferential.

Interestingly, many Americans who have lived in China have felt quite uncomfortable with this special treatment. They come from a culture that stresses freedom, self-reliance, informality, and equality of opportunity, and many have chafed under treatment that appears to violate these values and to deny their prerogatives as independent adults.

An American at home would suggest specific changes, register a complaint, or, if necessary, insist that his or her rights be respected. But this type of assertiveness is not recommended in China, for it would cause the American to lose face by being perceived as acting selfishly and disrespectfully. Chinese culture does not prepare its members to expect individuals to boldly state and pursue their uniquely personal needs and desires.

The Chinese belong to a collectivist culture, one in which mutual dependence rather than individual initiative is highly valued. An individual's well-being is thought to be best looked after by the other members of his or her primary groups, especially the family and the work unit. This is not to say that the Chinese have no personal concern for their own welfare. But if they were to pursue their individual goals with the assertiveness that often characterizes the behavior of Americans, they would break the unwritten rules that govern human interaction in the People's Republic. As we mentioned in chapter 7, the Chinese word for individualism, *gerenzhuyi*,* actually serves as a popular term for selfishness.

Guests as Members of Primary Groups

A significant contrast between the two cultures helps to illuminate the way in which Chinese hosts treat their guests. In the United States, members of a primary group tend to request assistance from each other. In China, members of a primary group tend to offer assistance to each other. The heart of the matter lies in who takes the initiative in determining that help is needed. In China, the initiative usually comes not from the one who needs help but from fellow group members whose care and concern predispose them to be alert to signs of need and even to situations that may lead to need in the future. In the United States, the initiative usually comes from the person who wishes to receive the help. Being offered assistance or protection when one has not directly requested it can be an embarrassment for an American, because such an offer may be viewed as an affront to one's self-reliance.[1] (Of course, there are exceptions, such as in the case of obvious disaster or in parent-child and other dependent relationships; in these cases, help is freely offered.)

Guests in China are usually treated as though they were members of the host's primary group; Chinese hosts therefore feel a keen sense of responsibility for their guests' welfare and happiness. A host's responsibility is discharged not merely by providing help when it is clearly needed but by actively and continuously protecting the guests from embarrassment, harm, loneliness, or the curiosity of outsiders. Guests who are Chinese expect this kind of treatment; they are comfortable in this dependency relationship and take this especially solicitous care as a compliment. But American guests often bridle

---

* For guidance in pronouncing Chinese words, see Appendix A.

at such care, sometimes even wondering whether it is an attempt to keep them under constant surveillance. The Americans' unhappiness is compounded by the fact that the meaning Chinese and Americans give to words such as *harm*, *embarrassment*, and *loneliness* can differ considerably.

To make matters worse, most Chinese are sensitive to the fact that their nation is still very much a developing country that lacks the products of modern technology, material comforts, and chic styles associated with the developed world. They assume that American and other Western guests will not be pleased to come into direct contact with the less seemly aspects of Chinese daily life. As part of their protective concern, they may attempt to keep their guests separated from everyday life in China. It matters little that the guests are eager to experience the "Real China." The duty of the host is to prevent embarrassment and displeasure, so he or she ensures that the guests will focus on China's model aspects. Understandably, they also have the desire to show family, community, and homeland in as favorable a light as possible.

The Dengji System

Typically, guests from abroad are housed in segregated living quarters, buildings used primarily by foreigners and overseas Chinese. Arrangements may be made for them to take most or all of their meals in cafeterias or restaurants where superior food is routinely served and where Chinese guests are admitted only by special arrangement. In addition there is the *dengji* system, which requires that most Chinese entering a guest house, dormitory, or apartment building reserved for foreigners must give information about themselves at the gate or in the lobby.[2] Consequently, the Chinese tend to be inhibited about making frequent visits to foreign residences. Americans in China occasionally cite the dengji system in support of their belief that Chinese authorities wish to prevent them from corrupting the values of ordinary Chinese in the local community.

Two points should be kept in mind when evaluating the dengji system. First, in any culture where hosts have traditionally felt keen responsibility for their guests' security, it is reasonable to have a system whereby the host can, if necessary, learn the identities of those who are going into the guests' living quarters. Second, all foreigners on extended assignments in China can leave their quarters and move about among the Chinese people in their community, including visiting them in their homes, virtually without restriction and without having to account for their whereabouts.

Americans tend to view the dengji system as objectionable in principle, but most of them eventually learn to coexist with it in practice.

Obtaining Personal Assistance

As a sojourner in China, you will face situations in which you need assistance from a Chinese person. These instances are not necessarily troublesome. As in any country, there are people in China who are designated as helpers for foreigners and other newcomers.

If you are at a hotel that expects its clientele to include tourists, there is a good possibility that the person at the front desk and perhaps even the manager speak English sufficiently well to respond to most requests routinely presented by travelers. Some of the newer and smaller hotels have interpreters on their staff whose assistance you can request if necessary. You are less likely to find that the switchboard operator speaks English, so if you have some need or problem, go to the front desk instead.

Most of the larger cities have Friendship Stores, which were originally organized to provide imported goods for resident foreigners and Chinese souvenirs for foreign tourists. Shop assistants at such stores will almost certainly speak English reasonably well, and many are helpful.[3] You can ask them about matters other than the merchandise, such as directions in the central city area.

Your Chinese work unit will most likely have assigned one
of your Chinese colleagues to interpret for you and to assist
you with various trivial and not-so-trivial problems. This
colleague, who is usually a junior member of the staff, will be
eager to help you. Rely on him or her as your first recourse
when problems arise.

Your Chinese work unit will almost certainly have a
waiban, or foreign affairs office. (At some universities, the
office that deals with foreign students is known as the *liuban*.
Foreign companies are unlikely to have a waiban; their human resources department functions in a similar manner.)
One of the principal responsibilities of this office is to look
after your welfare and deal with your requests. The junior
colleague discussed in the previous paragraph is probably
assigned to the waiban. One of your top priorities after your
arrival should be to develop a good working relationship with
the staff members at your waiban, some of whom will speak
English. Low-level officials such as these may not have much
power in the bureaucratic structure, but they can help matters go your way and are more likely to do so if you have good
personal relations with them.

It is unrealistic for you to expect that your waiban will be
able to banish every problem you bring to its attention;
American expatriates in China report a variety of experiences with their respective waiban—some good, some bad,
some indifferent.[4] But a sensible way to start out is to assume
that your concerns regarding living and working arrangements, intracity and intercity travel, and health and general
welfare will be dealt with by the staff at your waiban. Keep in
mind, however, that certain of your concerns will be wholly
the responsibility of the department, division, or other work-
related section to which you are assigned.

It is reasonable to present a minor request to the waiban
staff by speaking with them, but if you have an especially
important request, or if you have a number of requests, present
them in writing as well as orally. Written requests are likely

to receive more attention from the waiban staff, especially if (as is often true at the larger work units) they are constantly dealing with dozens of matters large and small. Do not hesitate to follow up on important requests by dropping in to the waiban office occasionally to ask how things are going. But during these brief visits, do not make yourself unpopular when things are not progressing efficiently by becoming visibly annoyed or by openly criticizing either individual staff members or the entire Chinese socialist system.

If you have an important problem that needs a solution and you know that it is beyond the usual range of responsibilities of both your waiban and your departmental supervisor, your best recourse is to communicate directly with one of the top officials of your work unit. Fortunately, it is entirely possible that you will have met at least some of the top officials at the opening banquet given in your honor. Use the waiban as your intermediary when making contact with one of these officials; otherwise, the waiban staff may assume that you have secretly gone over their heads. You may seek an appointment to speak personally with an official, or you may communicate with him or her in writing. If you speak directly with the official, you should also present a brief written statement of the problem. If the official's English is poor, take along your junior colleague to do the interpreting (unless the matter is confidential).

The time will come, sooner or later, when you find yourself on the street and in need of directions. Do not despair. Most Chinese are quite willing to help a foreigner with directions or with other minor requests. The following guidelines should facilitate your obtaining assistance under these circumstances.
1. Foreseeing that you are on your way to an unfamiliar location, take along a piece of paper with the address (and name, if there is one) written in English and in Chinese characters. Also, if possible, take along a map on which you have noted the location. Then, if you become lost, show these items to a passerby.

2. If you know that you will have other routine requests while on the street, carry the English and Chinese written versions with you and use them as indicated above. Incidentally, public toilets are ubiquitous in China except in Shanghai and Guangzhou (Canton); Chinese characters that you will soon learn to recognize are *nü* and *nán*, for women and men, respectively.

3. Try to approach a younger person when asking for assistance. They are often more responsive to requests, less shy, and more likely to be studying (or recently to have studied) English. Traffic policemen can also be relied upon to be responsive to your requests, though very few of them will speak any English. Or enter a large hotel and seek help at the front desk.
4. Learn to use a polite Chinese phrase, *Mafan ni*, to get the attention of a stranger on the street or of an attendant in a shop. *Mafan ni* is the equivalent of "Excuse me" in English.

Modesty in Dress and Self-Decoration

The international news media still focus on the relaxation of dress norms among the Chinese, but the fact is that almost all the photographs accompanying such articles are being taken in Beijing, Shanghai, Guangzhou, and a few other large or coastal cities where Western influence has been comparatively strong. During balmy weather in such locations, one can definitely see colorful T-shirts, jeans, and skirts, especially on younger Chinese. But change is not occurring nearly as rapidly as these reports seem to indicate. Many Chinese men in smaller towns and rural areas continue to dress in unostentatious, serviceable Mao jackets—which in China are called Sun Yat-sen jackets—and trousers of gray or dark blue. Women, especially younger women, tend to wear something more colorful.

The tendency to conform to a modest standard of dress is strong in China. Even on the boulevards of the largest cities, it is unusual to see miniskirts on women or the shorter versions of short pants on men or women. A woman wearing a sundress or other garment with a bare back or décolletage will attract much attention. With the exception of bathing suits at the beach or pool, any style of clothing revealing (on members of either sex) large amounts of skin that is normally covered will be considered unbecoming or worse by many Chinese.

Americans in the larger cities should be prepared for a curious exception to the general rule stated above. In warm weather, young Chinese women are often seen wearing blouses of such flimsy material that they reveal whatever is underneath. What is underneath is almost always a brassiere. Nevertheless, from an American male's point of view, the effect is sexually provocative as well as striking in the extent to which it exceeds the propensity of American women to reveal their upper torso and underclothing. The explanation of this seeming paradox is this: to the Chinese, baring skin that is normally covered is offensive or provocative; but skin covered by anything, even see-through material, is neither offensive nor provocative.

We do not recommend see-through blouses for American women in China, even in the warmest weather; rather, we suggest that American women dress in a manner that would be considered tasteful and modest in the United States. There is no necessity for them to eschew bright colors or fashionable styles, but they should definitely ensure that their shoulders, back, and chest are covered and that their hemlines are not above the tops of their knees. Socks or nylon stockings may be worn or not worn, according to personal taste. In winter, American women may find that they wish to imitate Chinese women by wearing slacks instead of skirts or dresses.[5]

Chinese men who work in offices and other indoor locations generally dress more comfortably than similarly employed American men. Neckties are worn only on those few formal occasions when a Western-style suit or sports coat is thought necessary. Three-piece suits are rare among the Chinese. However, men who work in Chinese banks, import/export companies, and joint-venture and other foreign-owned companies tend to wear Western suits.

Coping with Time-Use Differences

Time-use patterns of well-educated urban Chinese are similar to those of Americans and are becoming more so, but the traditional Chinese way of using time is unlike that of most Americans. Misunderstandings and annoyance are the likely outcome when these time-use patterns clash.

One of the biggest headaches of many Americans in China involves eleventh-hour invitations or notifications of schedule changes that they receive from Chinese acquaintances. For example, on Saturday evening you may find yourself invited to Sunday lunch. Or on Tuesday afternoon you may be told that your two o'clock class the following day has been rescheduled to four o'clock. These invitations and notifications are typically presented in a way that suggests that the possibility of your declining is not even remotely anticipated. You may find out, for example, that the family inviting you to Sunday lunch has already purchased the food; you may be told that the new class meeting time has already been announced to your students.

What should you do under these circumstances? Begin by trying to suppress your natural tendency to feel enraged over the "thoughtless" behavior of your Chinese hosts. You are not being invited to the Sunday lunch as a second-string substitute for a more preferred guest who is not able to attend. You are not being singled out for special antagonism by your department chairperson. Rather, you are being dealt with in a typically Chinese fashion by people who are only now becoming acquainted with the Western habit of keeping a daily diary and of working out intricate schedules for themselves days or even weeks in advance. Many of your Chinese acquaintances would not be annoyed by these invitations because, in fact, they would be able to comply without upsetting any plans.

Our advice is this. If you are physically able, comply with the eleventh-hour invitation or notification. If you are not physically able—let's say, for example, you have a definite plan to be on the train to Xi'an at the time of the luncheon or lecture—apologize for not being able to comply and explain why you cannot. Point out, too, that if you had only known a certain number of days or weeks in advance, you would have been able to adjust your schedule. After all, Chinese should become aware that Westerners make definite plans well in advance.

One additional time-use difference must be mentioned. There is no concept of "party"—an informal festive gathering—in traditional Chinese culture. It is quite common in the United States for someone to give a party to which people are expected to come and depart across a range of times. These events typically do not include a sit-down meal, thus freeing those who plan to attend from having to arrive by a certain time. People come and go as they please and spend most of their time at the party standing up and talking to a variety of other attendees one after another. This type of social gathering is only now beginning to become known in China, as is the extremely flexible, individual-oriented, time-use pattern associated with it. When you are invited to a social event in China, you are expected to arrive punctually and to depart at the same time that other guests leave. (Most Chinese are uncomfortable when they first attend a stand-up-and-circulate type of social gathering.)

Finally, we must highlight a fundamental difference between time-use patterns in China and the United States:

many Chinese are not as preoccupied as Americans with the efficient use of their time. For example, the time-is-money mentality of many Americans—the habit of paying less attention to the warm and humane aspects of social intercourse and more attention to the efficient completion of whatever productive task is at hand—is alien to many Chinese. (Among professionals and entrepreneurs, however, time tends to be valued as much as in the West.) You might find that the importance given to the development of warm and durable human relationships in China is quite refreshing. Some of your compatriots have in fact found it difficult to return to the rat race.

A Few Suggestions about Queuing

American residents of China sometimes give the impression that the Chinese never line up for any reason, that an unruly, flailing swarm of humanity can be found in front of every conceivable kind of ticket window, check-in desk, and other place where goods or services are dispensed. Americans who describe the Chinese in this way are venting their frustration with situations in which they have indeed encountered pushing and shoving. They have not noticed the many other situations that meet their expectations, those where the Chinese, with as much docility as Americans (if not the British), stand in line—sometimes lines that are incredibly long.

In fact, queuing is the general expectation among the Chinese. They expect to stand in line for all sorts of services and do not expect anyone to break into the queue, regardless of their age or rank. In general, therefore, this feature of Chinese time use should not pose a continual adjustment problem for Americans.

It is true, nonetheless, that queuing is observed less in some localities than in others and that it is rare throughout China in certain special circumstances. Two that are likely to annoy foreigners concern boarding trains and passing through customs at large airports.

If you are facing a nonqueuing situation in the company of a Chinese acquaintance, the best course is to ask him or her to obtain the tickets, information, or whatever. Usually, asking won't be necessary, but the other person will generally insist on bearing the cost—which you should accept with gratitude in cases where the cost is low.

If you are facing a nonqueuing situation alone, there is really no recourse but to wade in. Body contact cannot be avoided. Forget the queuing etiquette you learned as a child because, frankly, nice guys will finish last. Wedge into the crowd, and, holding the necessary money in your hand, force your arm toward the ticket window. If you know the Chinese hand symbols for numbers—which are not like typical American hand symbols—use them to communicate nonverbally with the clerk.

Additionally, we must discuss the boarding of buses and trolleys in urban areas of the PRC. During rush hours, embarking and disembarking from these vehicles can actually be dangerous, given the total disorganization of the process and the large number of people involved. We suggest that you avoid these means of transportation during morning and evening rush hours.

Accepting, Refusing, and Giving Invitations

Foreigners in China typically receive three types of invitations: (1) to relatively formal institutional events, (2) to relatively informal departmental events, and (3) to private gatherings.

The formal institutional events are typically banquets to honor arriving or departing colleagues or to mark special occasions such as Spring Festival. These are viewed as important social occasions by the Chinese; they dress well for them, and so should you (though this doesn't necessarily mean formal attire such as a tuxedo). Respond verbally to a verbal invitation; respond verbally or in writing to a written invitation. If you cannot attend, be sure to send regrets and offer an explanation.

Informal departmental events bring together people in your office or department and, often, their family members as well. These are frequently picnics and other kinds of outings. The invitation may be verbal, though often an open invitation will be posted on the departmental bulletin board. Respond verbally in either case.

Personal invitations to attend a small, private gathering in a home or restaurant will almost always be made verbally and should be replied to verbally.

Reciprocity for institutional and departmental banquets and other large events is not expected from individuals, but you should extend some form of reciprocity for personal invitations. For example, a foreigner who is leaving China might give one large dinner party for all those who have entertained or assisted him or her. For large occasions such as this, written invitations are appropriate, although you may certainly reinforce them verbally when the opportunity arises. For smaller occasions involving two or three Chinese acquaintances, a verbal invitation is quite acceptable. Senior officials, however, should receive a written invitation.

Americans sometimes say things to each other—such as "Let's get together soon"—that are expressions of goodwill rather than genuine invitations. The Chinese rarely do this. If one of your Chinese acquaintances talks about getting together, his or her statement should be taken at face value. If you say "Let's get together soon" when trying to demonstrate positive feelings toward a Chinese acquaintance, you may find an unexpected visitor at your door within the next few days, or you may cause hurt feelings because you have not followed through with a precise invitation.

Lending and Borrowing

If you borrow something from a Chinese acquaintance, make a point of returning it at the time you said you would. Most Chinese feel extremely reluctant to remind someone about something he or she has borrowed; having to ask can cause embarrassment, a strained relationship, even loss of face. If you do not return the borrowed item, the acquaintance will probably feel resentful.

When you lend something to a Chinese acquaintance, establish when it should be returned; the date should be in the near future, say, one or two weeks hence. Make a note in your date book for that day, and if the item is not returned at that time, do not hesitate to ask about it the next time you see the borrower. We give this advice because the items you lend to a Chinese may be valuable commodities in the community and thus may be circulated by the borrower to friends and colleagues. Books, especially, are treasured in China; if you have a small library, you may want to set up a lending system in which people sign their names and promised date of return. This may seem like too much trouble or too formal a process among friends, but the chances that you will be able to regain possession of your property diminish as time goes by because of the propensity of the Chinese to share items in their possession with friends and colleagues.

As in the United States, lending and borrowing money, especially in large amounts, is inadvisable because it tends to complicate relationships. If you feel it is necessary to lend a small amount of money to a Chinese acquaintance, think of it as a gift; but if repayment occurs, accept it. Conversely, if you absolutely must borrow a small amount of money from a Chinese friend, make a point of repaying it at your earliest opportunity.

Gift Giving among the Chinese

Occasions for Giving Gifts

Among most Chinese from the People's Republic, gift giving is associated with the following occasions:

1. Attending a birthday celebration
2. Visiting a sick person at home or in the hospital
3. Visiting relatives or good friends during Spring Festival, Mid-Autumn Festival, and New Year celebrations
4. Attending a wedding
5. Arriving for a lunch or dinner given by an individual with whom one is not on very close terms
6. Returning from a long domestic or foreign journey
7. Thanking an individual for a special service or kindness
8. Thanking an institution for hospitality rendered in the course of a brief visit (such as during a study tour)

The Chinese tend not to celebrate birthdays, the exceptions being older people's birthdays that are multiples of ten: 40, 50, 60, 70, 80, 90, 100. The higher the number, the more important the celebration. (Under Western influence, young people in major coastal cities of China have started celebrating each other's birthdays.) If you are invited to a birthday party in China, by all means bring a typically American gift of some kind.

When the Chinese have occasion to visit a sick friend or relative at home or in the hospital, they most often bring food or drink that promotes health, such as fresh or canned fruit, cakes, or tonics. If you are in China, bring an American-made gift associated with health if you can.

During Chinese festivals, adults give money to the children in their families; traditionally, the money is put in a red envelope or wrapped in red paper. Adult family members within the same household do not give presents to each other, but when visiting, adults often bring small presents for each other. If you are invited to a home in China during one of the Chinese festivals, bring toys or games for the younger children and some American coins wrapped in red paper for the older children. Bring something from the United States for your host and hostess as well.

At a wedding dinner, the Chinese traditionally give money or a gift to the bride and groom; this exchange normally occurs via an intermediary when the guest arrives. If you are invited to a wedding in China, do not give money; give a present of American origin such as kitchenware or house-wares.

When you are invited for lunch or dinner at a restaurant, you need not bring anything. But if you are invited to have dinner at someone's home, it is appropriate for you to bring a bottle of wine, flowers, or something you have brought from the United States. If there are children in the family, it would be a good idea to bring something for them as well.

If you are a resident in one locality in China and go on a tour of various other regions, do not feel obligated to bring presents back for your Chinese friends and neighbors. (An exception might occur, however, if you visit a very remote area of China that they would be unlikely to visit them-selves.) If during your sojourn in China, however, you return briefly to the United States for some reason, it would be appropriate to bring back some small items for your best Chinese friends. This could be an occasion to return with perishable food items to give as presents, since you should be able to distribute them within a few days of returning.

When you want to thank an individual who has rendered you a special service or kindness, make a careful gift selec-tion. Food or drink is not appropriate; something durable and especially useful to the person in question should be offered. For example, if the recipient is a teacher of English as a foreign language, he or she would probably be thrilled to receive one or more audio books selected from English-lan-guage literature.

If you are on a study tour of Chinese institutions and are hosted at each one for only a few days, it is appropriate for you to bring gifts for the top officials of the institution during the closing banquet. Since such gifts are from institution to institution (rather than from individual to individual), it is appropriate that they be comparatively expensive and that they be memorable rather than practical. Large, hardcover coffee-table books of photographs or art from the United States are good presents, as are larger examples of handicrafts or artwork such as sculpture. Items that include the insignia of your home institution are certainly appropriate. For individual Chinese from the hosting institution who are attending the banquet, bring smaller items such as paperweights, medallions, lapel pins, or mugs inscribed with your home institution's insignia.[6]

How the Chinese Accept a Gift

The traditional Chinese practice when exchanging gifts is quite different from that of Americans. The Chinese are taught as children that in order to show modesty and avoid any suggestion of personal greed, they should decline two or three times when offered a present. What usually occurs, then, is a seesaw battle in which the gift is offered and refused, offered and refused, offered and refused—but finally accepted with appropriate expressions of appreciation. The gift is not opened, though; rather, it is tucked away in a pocket or left on a table until the giver has departed. Then, and only then, is the parcel opened. One interpretation of this practice of not opening gifts upon receiving them is this: the receiver is preserving the face of the giver by avoiding any possibility of evaluating the gift in the presence of the giver and others.

When confronted by the seesaw battle, Americans must not conclude that the intended recipient feels unfriendly toward them or that their act of giving is not appreciated. Chinese modesty dictates such behavior, and the role of the giver is to keep on trying. And when Americans see that their gift is accepted but left unopened, they likewise should not reach any negative conclusions about the motives or politeness of the recipient. These behaviors are simply the Chinese acting in a Chinese manner.

There is always a very remote possibility that a Chinese person genuinely intends, for some reason, to refuse a present that is being offered by an American. Polite refusals tend to be carried out in a friendly, rather ritualistic manner, whereas the rare genuine refusal would be executed with considerably more firmness and seriousness of purpose. If you pass the fourth cycle in the seesaw battle with no indication that the intended recipient is going to yield graciously, you should consider the possibility of ceasing to offer the gift. But this rule should not be interpreted rigidly, since there are a few Chinese who will continue through more than four cycles of ritual refusal. If you sense that continued refusal is ritualistic, one alternative is to simply leave the gift on a table.

Western rules of etiquette are making increasing inroads in China. An American located in one of the larger cities near the eastern coast of China could offer presents to Chinese acquaintances over a period of a year or more without coming across the traditional Chinese patterns. The Chinese in these areas are quite likely to accept the gift on the first offering and to open it immediately.

What should you do when you are offered gifts by the Chinese? Observe your own cultural practices. If you are offered gifts by peasants or others in relatively remote areas of China, however, it might be best to refuse three times before accepting and then open the gift when you are alone.

Problems Associated with Expensive Gifts

Although it is true that most Chinese people do not give, and do not expect to receive, expensive gifts, cases do arise when such gifts are exchanged. For most purposes, any item valued in the PRC at over five hundred yuan (about U.S. $60.00) would be considered expensive by most Chinese.

There are two possible motives for the giving of expensive gifts. One is that the giver wishes to demonstrate the great significance attached to his or her relationship with the recipient. The other is that the giver wishes to obligate the other person to reciprocate at some future date either by returning a present of roughly equal value or by performing a significant favor for the giver. (See the discussion of guanxi in chapter 7.)

Our advice to anyone who lives or works with the Chinese is that they assiduously avoid giving or receiving highly expensive gifts, for an exchange of such items will probably involve an ongoing series of obligations that they will find burdensome if not downright troublesome. For example, if an American accepts an obviously expensive gift from a Chinese friend, the American may find the friend some years later asking him or her to make arrangements—possibly including financial assistance—for the friend's son or daughter to attend an American college.

Direct refusal of a gift is a fearful thing to do in any culture and perhaps especially so in Chinese culture, where face-consciousness plays a major role. Nevertheless, expensive gifts must be refused. We have no certain formula for carrying off such a refusal with grace and dignity except to counsel that you attempt somehow to reject the gift without appearing to reject the giver. One approach you might try is to shift the blame for your refusal to the policies of your employer: "You're wonderfully kind and generous, but my office [school] doesn't permit us to accept such valuable gifts. I'm terribly sorry." Embarrassment and loss of face might be an outcome of such an encounter, and a friend could be lost forever, but these unhappy consequences must be tolerated in the knowledge that acceptance is likely to lead to consequences of equal or greater unhappiness later on.

Being Entertained at a Meal

At a Restaurant or Faculty Club

Shortly after arriving at your destination in China, you will almost certainly be invited to a banquet in a restaurant or, if you are at a university, at the faculty club. This occasion is the welcoming banquet given for you and perhaps for other recently arrived foreigners by your host organization, counterpart organization, or danwei.

Both men and women should appear at such an event dressed much as they would when appearing at their office for a meeting with people they wish to impress. If it is extremely hot, seasonally appropriate garments are likely to be worn by the Chinese and may also be worn by guests. (More stringent rules may apply to diplomats and high government officials.) If in doubt, ask a Chinese acquaintance what type of dress will be appropriate.

The general rule is that guests are not required to bring gifts of any kind to a luncheon or dinner banquet. The single exception is in the case of touring visitors who are being hosted by the danwei for only two or three days; they should bring gifts to the banquet for distribution during their speeches and toasts toward the end of the meal. It is quite adequate for the visitors to present a gift to the principal host alone, but it is not wrong for them to distribute token gifts to all the Chinese who are present.

Proper seating of guests according to presumed seniority is important, so wait for your host to seat you. (Name cards are provided at some formal affairs.) At less formal banquets—these are more likely to be luncheons—the host may announce that there is no formal seating arrangement.

At many formal banquets, the liquor served for toasting purposes is often *maotai*, a highly prized and pungent brew produced in the southwest of China. Some Americans find Chinese liquor unacceptably strong; if you are among them, you may indicate that you prefer not to drink liquor by

turning your thimble-sized liquor glass upside down. You
need not toast with maotai or any other beverage you find
objectionable, but you must join in all toasts using some
beverage; not to do so would be rude.[7]

At a House or Apartment

You are not likely to be invited for a meal at a Chinese
colleague's house or apartment until a personal relationship
has been forged over a period of time. Being invited to a
Chinese home for a meal may indicate that the host feels his
or her relationship with you is close or that he or she wants
relations to become closer.

The first time you are invited, bring an inexpensive present
from the United States; if the family includes children, bring
small gifts for them also. Upon entering the home, you will
be introduced to family members with whom you are not
acquainted. Soon you will become aware that your host is not
helping you remove your outer garment. If you remove it by
yourself and ask what to do with it, your host might not give
you an adequate response. The explanation is that Chinese
people usually do not take off their outer garments upon
entering a home because the inside temperature is generally
similar to the outside temperature. Consequently, some Chinese hosts have never determined what guests ought to do
with their coats or sweaters. If your host seems unsure about
what you should do with such items, leave yours on a chair or
table in an obscure corner of the room.

If your principal host is the husband, the wife will be the
one working in the kitchen; if your principal host is the wife,
the husband might be the one in the kitchen. Since the
preparation of a Chinese meal requires frenzied activity within
the last hour or so before the meal begins, the cook is likely
to be out of sight much of the time. If he or she has a seat at
the table, it will be the one closest to the kitchen. Americans
are accustomed to waiting to eat until all present are seated
and served, but this expectation cannot be met when a large

meal is being prepared in a Chinese home. Don't insist on waiting until the cook is ready to eat.

You should make appreciative comments about the food and the hospitality, but be prepared for the host and the cook to apologize for various inadequacies; self-deprecation is considered good manners by the Chinese. Your response should be to reassert graciously that the meal is plentiful and delicious.

Rid yourself of any egalitarian convictions that might impel you to offer to help the family with the dishes. This is not done in China.

Hosting a Banquet or Other Meal

Basic Considerations

If you wish to entertain Chinese (and Western) colleagues and acquaintances in a relatively formal Chinese manner, invite them for a full-course meal. This may be either in your living quarters or at a restaurant, faculty club, or other eating facility.

In preparing the guest list, consider people who are more or less similar to yourself in rank and status. This rule should have more stringent application when government officials or diplomats are involved but can be interpreted loosely in most other social circles.[8] The Chinese may feel uncomfortable and constrained if someone present at a dinner or luncheon is much higher or lower in status than the rest of those present. It is often a good idea to invite some Western acquaintances.

People you know well may be invited verbally, but others, including all government officials, should receive written invitations, even if you also invite them verbally. Advance notice of a week to ten days is usually necessary in the case of government officials.

In determining your seating plan, you must not ignore the pecking order, because your Chinese guests will be highly conscious of it. If you are the only host, the seat on your right must be reserved for the highest-ranking guest; the seat on your left is for the second-ranking guest. If you have a cohost, he or she should sit directly across the table from you. On the cohost's right will be the second-ranking guest; on your left will be the third-ranking guest; on the cohost's left will be the fourth-ranking guest. If interpreters are necessary, each may sit either between the host/guest pair or in the third seat (counting from the host). The latter alternative has the advantage of eliminating the necessity for the interpreter to swivel his or her head back and forth throughout the meal.

Five or ten minutes after everyone has commenced eating, offer an appropriate short speech as well as at least one toast. At formal affairs, and at all affairs at which the party is divided among several tables, you should stand when doing this. The toast may be to deeper friendship, improved cooperation, better trade relations, or whatever sentiment may be appropriate. A second toast could be offered in honor of the most senior guest. If there are two or three tables, walk to each one and offer a special toast.

At evening meals in the winter months, begin the dinner at about 6:00 and expect it to come to a close around 8:00. In the summer months, begin about 7:00 and end around 9:00. Ending a dinner at a later hour might cause your guests to have transportation difficulties.

At a Restaurant or Faculty Club

Faculty clubs at the larger universities and major restaurants in the principal cities are experienced in handling banquets. When making arrangements with the manager of such an establishment, you need to agree on the date and time, the number of participants, and the *biaozhun*, which refers to the "standard" or quality of the meal as reflected in its cost. The biaozhun is expressed on a per capita basis and varies from city to city and from restaurant to restaurant within a city. As a general rule applicable at the time this handbook was revised (1998), a biaozhun of about fifty yuan for each guest's food is adequate for a restaurant in small and inland cities, while a biaozhun of eighty to a hundred yuan is required for a restaurant in larger cities and those on the coast. Drinks add about 30 percent to the food bill. There is in some cases a standard service charge (often 15 percent); separate gratuities should not be given. The exclusive use of a room also adds another two to three hundred yuan.

If any of your guests are of sufficient stature to be driven to your banquet by chauffeurs who will await their departure, then you are obligated to provide food for them; estimate about thirty yuan for each one.

On the day of the affair, be at the restaurant well in advance of the time when the earliest guest is likely to arrive. If you do not meet your guests upon their arrival, your standing as host will plummet. Ideally, you should be stationed at or very near the door in order to welcome them. Similarly, at the end of the affair, bid each guest farewell at the door of the restaurant.

At Your Home or Apartment

If you are planning to invite Chinese acquaintances to your home for a meal,[9] you will need some assistance. It doesn't matter whether you hire help, rely on an expatriate friend, or expect your spouse to cook; your duties as host necessitate that you be with your guests. It is important, therefore, that you spend as little time as possible in the kitchen.

Upon arrival, offer your guests tea and any other drinks, alcoholic and nonalcoholic, that are readily available in your locality, plus appetizers that are common in either China or the United States. Avoid cheeses; many Chinese do not like them. Be sure that all guests have comfortable chairs in which to sit after they arrive. Help your guests feel at ease by circulating among them and talking informally. (You can help them feel more relaxed by ensuring that your own dress is rather informal.)

If at all possible, treat your Chinese friends to a Western

meal. Most will be interested and appreciative, just as you would be if a Chinese friend in the United States invited you to a typical Chinese meal at home. Your Western meal may be Western in all respects, such as beginning with soup and ending with coffee and/or after-dinner drinks. Be wary of salads, however; many Chinese are disinclined to eat raw vegetables.[10] Provide chopsticks alongside the Western cutlery. It's fine for you to urge your guests to "help themselves" if you explain that serving oneself is the custom in the United States. Be alert, however, for guests who feel shy about helping themselves; put food on their plates as would a Chinese host.

If you decide to serve a buffet, invite some Western friends who won't mind demonstrating the procedure of going through the line, helping themselves, and returning for additional helpings. (A demonstration is best; an explanation might sound patronizing.) Since a Western-style meal usually requires that food be cut after it is on individual plates, try to ensure that all guests can sit at tables; trying to cut food on a plate balanced on their knees could lead to a minor disaster. If table seating is not a reasonable alternative, be sure that all food is bite-sized.

Problems of Foreign Teachers at Chinese Universities

Eleventh-Hour Assignment Changes

Almost all Americans going to teach in China know in advance the title and general nature of the courses they will be teaching. Unfortunately, a few of them have their assignments changed by the time classes meet; in rare cases, the new assignment is made only a day or two before the first class meeting. (When this kind of change occurs, it usually involves a switch to a subject with which the teacher is at least moderately familiar.)

You can reduce the possibility that your assignment will be

changed at the last minute by being sure that your predeparture correspondence penetrates the levels of the university's bureaucracy to the point where you are communicating directly with the supervisor (probably the department chairperson) with whom you will be dealing on a daily basis. This person is far more likely to be able to give you accurate information than any of the other officials (such as those at the waiban) with whom you may be in correspondence.

Chinese universities often do not have the degree of specialization found at American universities. For example, if you teach eighteenth-century English literature in the United States, you will likely be asked in China to teach the history of English literature, especially if your Chinese students are undergraduates.

At most Chinese universities there is a serious lack of teaching material of all kinds. The well-stocked campus bookstore that you take for granted in the United States rarely exists in the PRC. A typical procedure is to have whole chapters of a single available textbook typed onto a stencil and mimeographed for the students' use. (Typing pools are maintained for just such purposes.) Photocopying is not encouraged due to its expense and the poor condition of the machines. Knowing this, you might be tempted to ship textbooks for all your students to China. Do not do so, however, unless you are certain that the agreement about what you will teach is not only ironclad but also was made with the departmental administrator to whom you will report.

If you do have your assignment changed after your arrival, you can and should take the matter up with your department chairperson. Point out that you are far more qualified to teach what you came prepared to teach. But do not become openly angry about an eleventh-hour change; anger will cause you to lose face and may permanently diminish you in the eyes of your professional colleagues.

162

Interacting with Administrators and Other Faculty

Most American professors expect to take complete responsibility for their courses: content, materials, teaching methods, and evaluation of students' progress. They are quite happy to fit into the overall objectives of an academic department, but once they are given the "big picture," they expect to work with virtually no supervision. A few American teachers in China find, however, that the content of certain courses is specified and that other aspects of what they do in the classroom are externally regulated to some extent. Some also find that their Chinese students raise objections to their methods or materials, usually in cases where the students believe they are not being adequately prepared for major examinations.

The American educational system is one of the most decentralized in the world. The Chinese system is highly centralized, part of a culture that strongly emphasizes the positive values of consensus and control. Even though most Americans who teach in China have as much professional freedom as they do at home, this freedom is to some extent a concession to their expertise. Chinese supervisors ordinarily expect to have a say in what goes on in classrooms.

Your teaching might be observed by administrators and colleagues much more often than is the case in the United States. These visits are most likely motivated by a desire to learn about your teaching methods or the content of your course; they are rarely a form of inspection. If your teaching is observed often, your professional peers are probably paying you a compliment.

Americans with experience in colleges and universities in the United States go to China with the experience-based expectation that an individual faculty member can expect to have access to the chairperson of the department and to participate in discussions of impending departmental decisions. Of course, informal discussions with colleagues and perhaps covert political maneuvering play a role in the decision-making process in American university departments, but

most decisions are eventually worked out in open consultation between the faculty and the person with authority over
the matter in question.

In Chinese institutions, decisions are made differently;
although formal meetings do occur, the decision-making process places much more emphasis on informal consensus building. In fact, many Americans eventually reach the conclusion that most decisions are finalized prior to formal departmental meetings. They also note that consensus building
tends to be a never-ending process; teaching loads and assignments as well as other academic responsibilities are more
or less constantly the subject of bargaining and exchanges of
favors outside of formal meetings.[11]

Two rather typical outcomes of these Chinese procedures
can prove annoying to the American professor. First, more
time is required to make decisions, even important ones, than
is usually the case in the United States. Second, an American
or other foreign professor is not likely to play a significant
role in most of the decisions that are made; this is a result of
his or her being looked upon more as an honored guest than
a key player in departmental affairs.

Some Advice about the Clash of Teaching Styles

Some Americans expect to reform certain aspects of Chinese
educational practice. Often this expectation does not exist
(or at least is not consciously in mind) prior to the teachers'
departure from the United States. But once they begin to see
the typical modes of teaching and learning on the Chinese
campus, they decide that Western ways are far superior and
try to bring about changes through discussions in departmental meetings and/or through critiques of their Chinese colleagues' classroom practices. They expect to persuade their
colleagues of the obvious practical benefits of progressive
Western pedagogical approaches.

We know that some Western educators are strongly convinced of the superiority of their methods. Nevertheless, we

believe that they will be overstepping their bounds if they are assertive in pressing Western methods on their Chinese counterparts. For thousands of years the Chinese have been successful in learning needed information and skills using traditional pedagogical procedures. It is presumptuous for outsiders to visit and, after a rather brief period of observation, set out to reform those procedures. Chinese educational practices work very well indeed with some kinds of material. For example, foreign languages are learned remarkably well using traditional Chinese methods. Tani Barlow and Donald Lowe have this to report regarding one Western language teacher in China.

> Our colleague Valerie has taught English as a second language for years in France and knows other professionals teaching in Shanghai. She tells us very funny stories about foreign experts' attempts to change what they see as outdated Chinese teaching methods. They cannot accept the obvious fact that Chinese students learn better if they can learn in their own way: start with rote memorization, grammar rules, sentence construction and then worry about conversation and shades of meaning, not the other way around. Valerie has observed that Chinese students learn to read, write, speak, and then comprehend aurally in exactly the reverse order stressed by Western pedagogy. The emphasis on grammar means students tend to neglect comprehension, but can easily construct very good sentences. It seems inexcusably formalistic to most foreign language teachers. But in our experience, these students speak English more fluently after four years of study than their counterparts in the U.S. speak Chinese.[12]

To a considerable extent, the Chinese are interested in learning about modes of teaching and learning in the West; there is no reason whatsoever why American and other foreign educators in China should not share their techniques with Chinese colleagues when requested. And most American teachers are free to try their preferred pedagogical approaches in their own classrooms in China.

Otherwise, however, we subscribe to a point of view well expressed by Ed Porter at the end of his review of foreign involvement in China's higher educational institutions. In the context of English language learning, Porter argues that

> the foreign teacher should look upon his or her Chinese colleague as an equal. Many problems promise easy solutions if the foreign teacher but asks a Chinese colleague for advice. The Chinese teacher knows the particular problems Chinese students face in learning English and can explain them to foreigners if they want to hear. Each should learn from the other's strengths to offset their weaknesses. The foreigner knows his or her language, and the Chinese knows his or her culture. Working together with this attitude can produce more profitable results.[13]

A Note about Audience Behavior outside of Classrooms

If your professional activities among Chinese people include the giving of formal presentations, you can expect many of your audiences to be reasonably similar in comportment to American audiences. But a large audience in China is capable of activity that is potentially distracting. If your presentation is irrelevant, patronizing, too difficult for them to understand, or just plain boring, some Chinese will simply get up and walk out. If audience members feel compelled to stay in spite of not being interested, they might talk with one another, walk around, stretch, or even fetch and drink tea. Chinese speakers seem not to be offended by such behavior and resolutely continue with their presentations (which they often read with head down, a fact that reduces their awareness of the goings-on in the audience). As an American, however, you are likely to find such behavior distracting if not objectionable. If you find yourself facing an audience that seems rude, remember that you are not being singled out for disrespect but are being treated as would any native Chinese speaker in similar circumstances.

Except as noted above, Chinese behavior in formal class-room situations tends to be passive, reserved, formal, attentive, and respectful, so you might expect that other audience situations in China would be more or less similar. In some cases, though, they definitely are not. In *Iron and Silk*, Mark Salzman tells a story that nicely illustrates this point.

After the touching of the [red velvet lining inside my cello case], they asked to hear the instrument. I tuned it up, waited until they were ready, and began to play Bach's First Suite for Unaccompanied Cello. The instant I drew the bow over the strings, the family started talking with one another, in full voice, mostly about the velvet. I thought perhaps I had mis-understood and they didn't want me to play, so I stopped. Gradually they became silent and looked at me. "Why did you stop?" I felt puzzled but started again. Right away they re-sumed their conversations, the children laughed and played with the case, and [one young man] initiated an arm wrestle with the third brother. When I finished the first movement, they looked at me again. "Is that all?" I must admit that I felt disappointed that their first exposure to the cello, and to Bach, was generating so little interest. But then I remem-bered what a Chinese friend had told me one night at a performance of instrumental music where the audience talked, laughed, spat and walked around during the show. I men-tioned to him that the audience seemed unbelievably rude, and he answered that, on the contrary, this showed they were enjoying it. He said that for the majority of Chinese who are peasants and laborers, music is enjoyed as a sort of back-ground entertainment and is intended as an accompaniment to *renao*, which means literally "heat and noise." *Renao* is the Chinese word for "good fun," the kind you might have at an amusement park in America, and noise and movement are essential to it.[14]

Interacting with Domestic Employees

Hiring and Compensating Domestic Help

Foreigners in China with children are the ones most likely to hire a domestic employee on a regular basis. Whether this person is a part-time baby-sitter or a full-time presence in the household who cooks and cleans as well as minds the children, she is called an *ayi*, a pseudokinship term meaning "aunt" (from the point of view of the child). In some of the provinces in the south of China, the most common word is *ama*.

To recruit an ayi (or even a domestic who only cooks and cleans), there are two possible procedures to follow. The first is to inquire locally among other expatriates, especially those who are about to return to their home country. They may have an ayi whom they would like to see employed by someone else before they depart. If that procedure does not identify someone quickly enough, you should then work through the waiban or human resources department of your employing institution or, if you are a diplomat, through the diplomatic services bureau. A few large foreign-owned enterprises have started to do their own hiring; if you work for such an organization, consult its personnel office.

If you do identify a suitable candidate by means of referrals from other foreigners, approach the waiban or services bureau to complete the arrangements. Even though you are primarily observing a formality, it might not be good politics to ignore these agencies. If you cannot identify a suitable candidate by means of referrals, you definitely should rely on these indigenous agencies. You should not attempt to make direct hiring arrangements with a Chinese domestic with whom you happen to be acquainted, because, as a recently arrived outsider, you run the risk of hiring someone whose background is questionable, who is not completely dependable, or who is unacceptable to your work unit.

Pay a domestic helper according to either the fixed rate set by the services bureau or the waiban or the rate that you and the domestic agree upon at the time of employment. If you expect to negotiate a rate with a potential employee, ask other expatriates about the range that prevails in your locality. If your agreement with your helper is a private one, you may consider giving him or her a raise after a year or perhaps six months of satisfactory service.

What you must not do, even for exceptional service, is to give gratuities or small gifts of money to your domestic helper (or to anyone in any service capacity). Tipping is considered an insult in China because it calls specific attention to the difference in rank and station between the giver and receiver of the tip, thus openly contradicting the ethos of equality. Instead of a tip, you may give a sizeable bonus to your domestic at some appropriate time during the year, such as during the Spring Festival. For example, if your domestic has been fully satisfactory, you might give her or him an extra month's pay on one of these occasions.

If you wish to say thank you in a less expensive way, give a small, nonmonetary gift to your domestic on the occasion of the Spring Festival or just prior to your departure. The gift should be something practical, inexpensive, and, if possible, from the United States. Before your departure, you have another opportunity to do something nice for your domestic: give him or her the most serviceable items of clothing that you do not want to haul back home. Your domestic will greatly appreciate this type of gift, although you can expect to go through the ritual seesaw battle before he or she accepts the clothing.

Maintaining Good Relations with Domestic Employees

The ethnic and cultural differences between you and your domestic helpers are likely to be unusually prominent, because they will not have had many opportunities to come into direct contact with Westerners. Chinese domestics typically come from a rural background where traditional Chinese values prevail. You should expect that they will offend you sooner or later by committing some sort of cultural faux pas. (And you might likewise offend them.) Prepare yourself mentally so that if this occurs, you can deal with the problem in a dignified, gentle manner.

Your domestic helpers are also likely to be very consciously aware of your elevated status in China. It really doesn't matter whether you are a high-ranking diplomat, a businessperson, a foreign expert, or an expatriate teacher—all of these are special from the point of view of Chinese domestics. They may have a strong tendency to maintain a distant, formal relationship with you, whereas it is important for you to deal with them warmly and personally.

Finally, even though the ethos of present-day China includes the notion that all types of productive work are equally respectable, the truth of the matter is that many Chinese still regard some jobs as more prestigious than others. Not surprisingly, domestic work is commonly looked down upon. (Taxi driving, however, tends to be admired for the driver's ability to yield a high income.) You should always remain sensitive to the fact that the work of your domestic helpers may be deprecated by some of their fellow Chinese.

Consequently, your domestic helpers are likely to be especially sensitive to how you treat them. They may interpret something you say inadvertently or in jest as a deliberate insult. They may view your concentration on your work or your momentary reticence or distraction as an indication that you cannot be bothered to speak with them. So it is important that you constantly make an effort to show them they are valued as human beings. This is particularly true if you employ an ayi for more than just occasional baby-sitting; an ayi who is in your house frequently should come to be treated more or less as a member of your family.[15]

You can forestall misunderstandings by having your guidelines ready, preferably in written form (largely for your own benefit), before your domestic first arrives. Unless you speak Chinese fluently, have a bilingual acquaintance join you on that day. Explain and demonstrate each point, focusing on the details that are important to you. For example, don't just say that the hardwood furniture is to be dusted twice a week; say that it must be dusted using such-and-such a product on the cloth, never water. Take time to demonstrate how you want specific tasks carried out.[16]

Little things can make a difference in promoting a positive relationship between you and your domestic. For example, find out how your helper is addressed by his or her peers. Most often, they will use *lao* or *xiao* as the common form of address. (These terms are discussed in chapter 2.) You should do likewise, regardless of the age difference between you. If you speak some Chinese, converse occasionally with your helper about his or her family and hometown, about local Chinese customs, or about the local gossip. Show your helper photographs of your own family and hometown in the United States. If your helper is an ayi, talk about the child who is the link between you and her. If you are taking Chinese lessons, get your helper to advise you on pronunciation and new vocabulary for items around the house. Informal contacts such as these will go far in furthering your relationship.

A Special Note about Child Care

When it comes to the raising and socialization of children, people everywhere tend to have strong opinions grounded in the basic values of their native culture, so it is likely that you and your ayi will have some very different ideas about how children are to be dealt with. One of your options is to allow your ayi to do things entirely her way. If that is not acceptable to you, you are free to expect your notions about child rearing to be complied with. But as an experienced adult (probably a mother) from another culture, your ayi may find it difficult to adjust to your preferences.

A few facts about Chinese child raising may help you

appreciate the types of disagreements that are likely to arise. Chinese parents tend to be more protective of infants and small children than are Americans. As small Chinese children grow a bit older, they are restricted in ways that seem odd or worse to Americans who are eager to see children develop self-reliance. Younger Chinese children are not allowed to roam around and explore on their own but are kept close to the adult who is tending them. Relations with parents, siblings, and other relatives are promoted; obedience to the father is stressed; freedom to establish close relations beyond the circle of family friends and nearby neighbors is limited. Also, Chinese children are inhibited from showing aggressiveness toward others. In sum, their training in the key Chinese values of family-centeredness, collectivism, and harmonious relationships begins on day one of their lives and continues for as long as they remain at home—which, in China, is until they are married and often longer.

Be patient with your ayi. Explain how you want your child dealt with and not dealt with, but don't expect that it will be easy for her to do things exactly as you require. People in all cultures often find it almost impossible to deal with children in a manner with which they don't really agree. Keep on explaining to her what you want done but be ready, too, to accept some compromises in areas that do not directly affect the physical and mental health of your children.

Social Aspects of Traveling

Intercity Travel

A major difficulty of intercity travel in China is that tickets are hard to obtain and that only in a few major cities can you get round-trip tickets. If your Chinese is not fluent, get help when making travel-related arrangements. If you wish to join a tour, you can approach your waiban or contact China International Travel Service (CITS) directly. If you wish to travel on your own, the easiest way is to make your bookings at the office of a travel agent at a big hotel; in this case expect to pay an extra twenty or thirty yuan for the booking. Finally, Chinese friends or colleagues may be willing to help you make plans or purchase tickets.

The most common means of intercity travel for the Chinese is by train. China has an extensive railway network with reasonably modern equipment—many steam locomotives in beautiful condition are still in service and intercity trains are usually speedy and dependable. There are four categories of quality on intercity passenger trains: hard seat, hard berth, soft seat, and soft berth. The two categories designated "hard" are roughly the equivalent of second class in other countries. The two categories designated "soft" are first class. Hard berth consists of six thinly padded cots stacked three to a wall in unenclosed compartments. Soft berth has four comfortable beds in each enclosed compartment.

Most Chinese travel by hard seat, making these carriages very crowded, sometimes even to the point of people standing shoulder to shoulder in the aisles. Seats are arranged face-to-face and human interaction is unavoidable. In the hard-berth carriages, direct contact is nearly as inevitable (the exception being that you may be able to isolate yourself in a second- or third-level berth). Traveling via hard seat or hard berth is one of the best ways to make direct, sustained contact with individual Chinese, who are more open to impromptu conversations with strangers while riding trains than during virtually any other common activity.

In soft-seat and soft-berth carriages you will find an unusual mixture of people, for these are preferred by native Chinese of high social standing, wealthy businessmen, overseas Chinese, and foreigners on tour. People are less likely to be talkative than in the hard carriages, but your chance of finding a fellow speaker of English is greater.

Commercial air service in China has been expanding, and there are now over a dozen airlines. There are direct flights from Beijing or Shanghai to many scenic places like

Huangshan, Hangzhou, and Zhangjiajie. Most airports, however, are crowded and delays much more frequent than in the
United States. What a foreign traveler finds most annoying is
that no explanations are given when such delays occur. Once
aboard a commercial airliner, the experienced traveler may
find that service is of marginal quality. Some flight attendants speak a little English and might be able to assist the
English-speaking traveler. Passengers may be from anywhere
in the world. Chinese passengers, mostly traveling on business, seem well disposed toward their foreign traveling companions. As on commercial airliners everywhere, extended
conversations among fellow passengers occur infrequently.

Intercity bus service exists in China, but it bears no comparison to Greyhound or Trailways or the superb intercity
services of Europe. Bus services typically operate between
smaller towns or between a city and its neighboring towns.
The passengers are usually crowded onto dilapidated equipment. People seem to be less talkative on Chinese buses than
on trains, perhaps in part because the all-facing-forward seating pattern discourages interaction. In general, bus tickets
are not difficult for a foreigner to obtain.

Travel within Cities

Transportation within large Chinese cities is limited for most
practical purposes to buses and trolleys, minibuses, taxis, and
bicycles. Only Beijing, Shanghai, Tianjin, and Guangzhou
boast subway systems, which are still limited in size. Public
bus and trolley service is frequent and regular, but the equipment is often in poor condition. During rush hours, the crush
upon entering and exiting often leads foreigners to fear for
their safety. But during nonrush hours, travel by bus or trolley
may be a pleasant alternative to walking or cycling. Fares are
very cheap, but most routes shut down an hour or two before
midnight. Trolleys and buses are usually staffed by a conduc-
tor, who sells tickets, as well as by a driver. It may be possible
to purchase monthly commuter tickets at certain locations.

In most major cities minibuses supplement the regular buses and trolleys. These often serve established bus stops and in some cases may be hailed from the side of the road. Minibus services typically operate between the downtown areas and certain outlying districts, sometimes including tourist attractions (which the Chinese also visit). Fares are slightly higher than those of buses and trolleys. There may also be special, modern bus services that cater to the needs of tourists and foreign employees. Some institutions employing foreign experts provide private bus service for special excursions as well as for daily commuting. There may be a public bus service for tourists between the downtown area and major sightseeing locations. Typically, fares are reasonable, seating is guaranteed, and equipment is new or nearly so.

Taxis are available in all major cities and in many smaller towns, but they are expensive. In cities such as Beijing and Shanghai, taxis are required to have meters, and each taxi has externally visible information regarding its fare. In other cities and in smaller towns, metered taxis are rare. When there is no meter, the fare must be negotiated in advance. Tolls are paid by the taxi driver and added to your fare. Tips are not necessary for taxi drivers.[17]

In large cities getting a taxi is not difficult. You may hail a taxi from the street, and except for morning rush hour or wet weather, you are likely to get one fairly easily. In smaller cities taxis tend to cluster around train stations, hotels, and locations where foreigners and others with sufficient funds are expected to be seeking transportation. At such locations the would-be rider usually enters a queue or, if there is no queue, simply walks to and enters the next available taxi. You may also telephone for a taxi, but you might have to wait a long time.

Taxis can be hired for a full day or other extended periods of time. The drivers seem not to mind the long waits that are inevitable as you go about your business at each stop along the way. You do not necessarily have to approach the taxi company in order to arrange for such a long-term engagement; an alternative is simply to approach a taxi driver and ask what his company's policy is regarding full-day hires.

Bicycles are everywhere in China. Large bicycle parking lots with attendants, where you can (and should) park your bike for a minuscule fee, are common sights. One way you can absorb the feeling of what it means to be an ordinary Chinese citizen is to join them in their two-wheeled commute to and from work and on all sorts of other errands. An ideal way to socialize with your Chinese acquaintances is to cycle with them to a tourist attraction or park. Ask a Chinese friend to assist you in obtaining a license for your bicycle, a process that can usually be completed by means of one trip to a local office. And don't worry what you will do if your bike has some kind of breakdown; little bicycle repair shops are ubiquitous.

Bicycling in China can be dangerous. Americans are not used to riding together with hundreds of other cyclists in their immediate vicinity. Cycle collisions occur even between experienced Chinese cyclists. In larger cities, some thoroughfares include special cycling lanes, but on most ordinary streets the cyclist feels very much at the mercy of automobiles, trucks, and buses (though these are far less numerous than in American cities). Another problem is that the roads are often rough, and it is not uncommon to suddenly come upon large potholes, depressions, or even a manhole with its cover ajar. Pedestrians occasionally step in front of cyclists with no apparent concern for their own safety.[18]

In major cities such as Beijing, Shanghai, and Guangzhou, car rental services are now available, but unlike in the West, they are seldom found at airports or train stations. Although procedure varies from city to city as well as from company to company, usually the renter places a deposit of several thousand yuan with the car rental agent. The actual car rental fee varies from three to four hundred yuan per day. You can rent a car for a week or a month, in which case the daily rate is lowered considerably. (In some cases, car rental companies are able to provide drivers as well as cars.) Regarding insurance, most policies cover 80 percent of whatever you have to pay for the damage in case of an accident; the renter pays 20 percent. Total insurance coverage is rare.

Preparing for Your Final Return to the United States

Presenting Farewell Gifts

The items that you give as farewell gifts need not necessarily be shiny new presents that you have kept wrapped up in the bottom of your suitcases. Your special friends and colleagues may be enormously satisfied to receive something that you have been using during your stay. An excellent example is the books that visiting professors use while teaching at Chinese universities. These are greatly coveted by Chinese professors and students in the same field; the fact that they are used makes no difference. Foreigners in business and the professions should consider making gifts of books describing Western management concepts and skills, or of other tools of the trade that they are using in China and can afford to leave behind.

One caution is warranted. If you wish to offer gifts to some of the same individuals whom you are also inviting to a farewell meal, do not distribute those gifts during that meal. Give your gifts on another occasion, preferably when you are alone with the receiver or at least in the company of only his or her immediate family.

You may be tempted to sell some of your belongings before departing from China. If so, sell them to other expatriates, not to the Chinese. Selling personal property to the Chinese involves risking bad feelings because of the haggling over the price or criticism by the colleagues of the Chinese over an aspect of the deal.

Preparing Yourself for the Return Home

Almost everyone expects that adjustment is not required when returning home. The experience of countless sojourners shows conclusively, however, that this common-sense expectation is often wrong. Cross-cultural researchers have found that the people who are most successful in adapting to life, work, and human relationships in an unfamiliar culture often have the greatest difficulty in readapting upon their return to their supposedly familiar home culture.[19]

Marcia Miller, an American teacher who has written movingly about her six-month struggle to readapt to her native Manhattan after a year of work in the remote Chinese city of Daqing, has drawn a useful analogy between jet lag and what she terms "culture lag." When one travels rapidly into a substantially different time zone, the body's physiological processes as well as the routine activities of eating and sleeping are upset by the out-of-synch sequence of daylight and darkness. Culture lag is analogous in many ways. When one travels to an unfamiliar culture, one's complex expectations regarding the patterns of everyday life—such as social etiquette, nonverbal behavior, and the development of relationships—are thrown into disarray. It requires time for a sojourner to sort out, both consciously and subconsciously, the new details and patterns that are characteristic of life and work in the new cultural environment.[20]

But if one remains long enough in the new culture, and especially if one becomes involved with indigenous people and events, one finally does catch up culturally. The strange details become so routine that they are no longer noticed; the unfamiliar patterns of life and work finally become familiar, confidently expected, even overlearned.

Anyone who is an experienced airline traveler knows that jet lag strikes regardless of whether one is flying to an unfamiliar culture or is flying home. Yet people typically expect that, after sojourning in a previously unfamiliar culture, they will have no difficulty with culture lag. They concede readily that their body's physiology will have adjusted to another time zone, but they do not accept that they will have adapted socially and psychologically to the patterns of the other culture. Do not make this mistake. Many expatriates have formed deep attachments to the Chinese people and their culture and have found readjustment to their home culture and community to be a protracted and somewhat painful process.

An effective step you can take to deal with culture lag (also known as "reverse culture shock" or "reentry") is simply to recognize in advance that it is quite likely to happen to you. By learning about reverse culture shock in advance, you can make some mental plans that will soften its impact. In addition, you can seek out fellow expatriates who have previously had the experience of returning home after a lengthy period of living and working in another culture. Finally, do a bit of reading. We recommend the evocative piece by Marcia Miller mentioned above as well as *The Art of Coming Home* by Craig Storti.[21]

Keeping in Touch after Your Return

Friendships and business relationships are looked upon by the Chinese as connections that should have, among other things, the quality of durability and even permanence. Try not to disappoint this expectation of the Chinese with whom you established the closest relations during your sojourn.

Keep in touch with your most valued Chinese friends and colleagues by means of a card or letter sent at least once a year. Some returned expatriates make the Chinese Spring Festival in February the occasion of their annual card or letter, and some go to considerable lengths to obtain traditional Chinese greeting cards. Such a gesture is no doubt appreciated by their friends back in China. We suggest, however, that you send typically American greeting cards to your Chinese friends during the Christmas/New Year season.

Finally, you may be tempted to mail packages containing items of one kind or another to your Chinese friends and colleagues. Be aware that your intended recipient is likely to have to pay a heavy import duty before taking possession of the package. These duties sometimes are so high (except on books, which are duty-free) that he or she might have to pay more than the actual cost of the item. Given the level of Chinese salaries, receiving your packages could prove to be a major financial burden for your friend.

Before you send any packaged item to China, we recommend that you consult by letter with the intended receiver to find out whether he or she may have to pay a heavy duty. If such an expense is likely, try to contact someone who will be traveling to China in the near future. If that person will agree to include the package in his or her luggage and then to mail it after arriving in China, your intended recipient will not have to pay any duties.

---

[1] Victor H. Li offers a useful way of conceptualizing this basic difference between Chinese and U.S. cultures. He writes:

> [In the United States], "leaving the person alone" is held to be one of the cornerstones of our social system and philosophic beliefs. The right of a person not to follow strictly the generally accepted norms of conduct is not a matter that is the legally enforceable business of another citizen. As this person deviates more and adopts a lifestyle increasingly annoying to the rest of the community, we still leave him alone. As the deviation increases, at some point he goes too far and a "crime" is committed. At that point, we do not leave this person alone, and the full majesty of the criminal law descends on him. Pictorially, it is like falling off the edge of a cliff. As the deviant wanders closer and closer to the edge, he is left alone. He suffers no penalty but also receives no help. When he steps over the edge, the fall is sudden and drastic.
>
> The Chinese take an approach entirely different from ours, however, concerning how these minor expressions of

unhappiness or antisocial tendencies should be handled. They do not leave the person alone at this stage. Quite the contrary, anyone who notices these expressions...is supposed to "help." If the deviant does not respond to the help and continues to wander further from the "correct path," the amount of help given is increased, both in quantity and in intensity. In the usual case, this help takes the form of peer pressure, ranging from a public discussion of the deviant's "problem" to offerings of suggestions and criticisms that grow increasingly pointed. Pictorially, rather than falling off the edge of the cliff, the Chinese system more resembles a gradual slide to the bottom, in which peer pressure increases as the deviation grows greater. Some recalcitrants, of course, will hit bottom, and they will be handled by the formal criminal process.... Still, it takes quite a bit of doing to hit bottom.

Victor H. Li, *Law without Lawyers: A Comparative View of Law in China and the United States* (Boulder, CO: Westview Press, 1978), 39, 45.

2 Some Chinese manage to evade dengji procedures by arriving in an automobile or dressing exceptionally well for their visit.

3 Although shop assistants in Friendship Stores tend to be courteous, assistants in other stores and shops sometimes are not. This problem is one that affects Chinese as well as foreign shoppers. In 1986 the Chinese People's Political Consultative Conference, an advisory body that convenes in Beijing from time to time, publicly complained about the rudeness and lack of attentiveness of the shop assistants in that city. But certain practices that Americans view as thoughtless or rude are acceptable in China. The Chinese say *xie xie*, or thank you, far less frequently than do most Americans, a fact as true of shop assistants as of Chinese in general. And Chinese assistants often seem to fling the change down on the countertop, a gesture easily interpreted by Americans as negatively motivated. However, a likely explanation is that the assistant is spreading the change out on the countertop to facilitate your counting it.

4 For a well-informed discussion about the variety of experiences that Americans living in China have had in dealing with their

respective waiban, see Karen Turner-Gottschang and Linda A. Reed, *China Bound: A Guide to Academic Life and Work in the PRC* (Washington, DC: National Academy Press, 1987), 45–48, 76–77, 109–10.

5 Winters can be bitterly, unremittingly frigid in China. Even in the southern part of the country, where there is no indoor heating, winters can be extraordinarily difficult. The Chinese deal with their cold winters by wearing layer upon layer of clothing. You will find that you must do likewise.

6 Following are thirteen suggestions regarding types of gifts that Americans could easily and relatively inexpensively bring to China.

Books: Bring English-language books for Chinese friends or acquaintances who know or are learning English. Paperbacks are fine. Greatly appreciated are fiction (especially the classics), contemporary nonfiction, poetry, children's books, art reproductions, photography (especially American scenes), reference works (such as dictionaries), Americana, scholarly books, and advanced English as a second language texts that stress idiomatic English. Avoid books with explicit references to sex or with pictures of nudes.

Tapes: Bring taped readings of English-language materials; these will be greatly valued by those who are learning or teaching English, especially if they come with a typescript of the reading. Tapes of American and other Western music—classical, contemporary, and especially folk (such as traditional ballads)—make good gifts.

Maps, poster and art prints: Bring high-quality maps of the United States or of portions of it, such as one of the major U. S. cities. Bring posters and art prints only if you can pack them in a way that will not necessitate folding and will prevent wrinkling.

Calendars: For gift giving during December and January, bring calendars with color photographs of American scenes or with color reproductions of American art.

Food: Bring nonperishable specialty foods that are well packaged in individual small quantities. Examples include chocolate bars for adults and hard candies for children; other possibilities include bouillon cubes and instant coffee.

Stamps: Some Chinese collect stamps and will appreciate a collection of U.S. postage stamps; these can be sorted into small plastic packages before you depart and are effortless to carry.

Clothing: Bring T-shirts imprinted with a slogan or cartoon identified with your region, locality, company, or university. Additional possibilities include baseball hats, neckties, scarves, and so forth.

Toys and games: Small toys, jigsaw puzzles, brightly colored marbles, uncomplicated games, playing cards, and cuddly teddy bears are among the gifts that are appropriate to give Chinese children. Word games will be popular with those studying English.

Souvenir items: Pencils with messages (such as "I Love New York"), pins celebrating a region of the United States. (such as a Kansas sunflower), notepaper with an appropriate message, and other small, inexpensive souvenir items should be included among your gifts.

Postcards: Postcards showing scenes of your hometown or region or of famous places in the United States are easy to carry and make quite appropriate gifts.

Kitchen items: Small convenience items for the kitchen such as can openers, vegetable peelers, egg beaters, and Tupperware containers are items that may appeal to Chinese, male and female, who are combining full-time employment with housekeeping.

Local handicrafts: If your region or locality is known for some kind of local handicraft that is lightweight and inexpensive, bring a number of these to give as presents.

Special suggestions: Post-It sticky notes, Liquid Paper, tubes of good quality hand cream, oversized paperclips, and hand towel sets are among the items that others have found to be appreciated by the Chinese. Certain items that you have reserved for your own use during your sojourn—books and tapes are prime examples—can be distributed as gifts in the weeks prior to your return home.

Do not bring for gift-giving purposes items that are already easily obtainable by Chinese. For example, ballpoint pens and pocket calculators of good quality are now widely available. Also avoid socially inappropriate gifts, which include any item that could be considered personal: jewelry for men or women, perfume or any other kind of cosmetics, soaps or items used for grooming the hair, outerwear other than the few items mentioned above, and, of course, intimate apparel of any description. Except in very unusual circumstances, such items should not be given as gifts by foreigners.

7 In unusual cases, the Chinese put pressure on anyone who is not inclined to toast with an alcoholic beverage. If you are subjected to such pressure, say (truthfully or otherwise) that you are under a physician's orders not to consume alcohol. Make clear your eagerness to join in the toast using any nonalcoholic beverage at hand.

8 If you are inviting guests from more than one work unit, it is especially important for you to ensure that all are of similar rank.

9 If your home or apartment is within a diplomatic compound, provide your guests with written invitations. These will be important for them upon arrival, as they will need to show them to the Chinese guards. Otherwise, you will probably have to go to the gate to identify them for the guards.

10 Inquire locally to obtain advice regarding the peeling and/or washing of any raw vegetables that you intend to serve (or to eat yourself). Regardless of what you do to cleanse raw vegetables, many Chinese will be reluctant to eat them because human feces is sometimes used as fertilizer in local gardens.

11 Turner-Gottschang and Reed, *China Bound*, 110, 117. For more thorough information, see their entire fifth chapter, "Teaching."

12 Barlow, Tani E., and Donald M. Lowe, *Chinese Reflections: Americans Teaching in the People's Republic*. New York: Praeger, 1985, 82–83.

13 Edgar A. Porter, "Foreign Involvement in China's Colleges and Universities: A Historical Perspective," *International Journal of*

Intercultural Relations, 11, no. 4 (1987): 382. Porter in turn cites this point of view as originating in J. Wu, "*Quchang Buduan*— A Chinese View of Foreign Participation in Teaching English in China," *Language Learning and Communication* 2: 114–15.

14 Mark Salzman, *Iron and Silk* (New York: Random House, 1986), 122–23.

15 For example, early in your relationship with your ayi, you should invite her to join your family during meals. Repeat this invitation several times to demonstrate that you are not merely being polite. If she insists that she would prefer to eat alone, allow her to do so.

16 An acquaintance of ours notes that expatriates should not assume that a Chinese domestic brings to the job a finely tuned knowledge about how to do things that Americans take for granted. He had all the shine permanently removed from his car by a well-meaning domestic who washed it with an industrial-strength version of Ajax or Comet.

17 Foreigners in China sometimes complain about overcharging by taxi drivers. (Different fares may apply in certain zones or at various times of day; drivers are able to change the rate used by the meter to calculate the fare, and some drivers inappropriately raise the meter's rate.) One way you can avoid being overcharged is to find out beforehand from a reliable third party how much you should expect to pay from point A to point B; then, at the end of the journey, pay that amount. Another way to avoid being overcharged is to negotiate the amount before the journey begins; this is possible, though, only if the taxi is unmetered. If you think you have been overcharged to a serious extent, pay what is requested after obtaining the number of the car and the name of the taxi company; you can then file a complaint with the company. The knowledge that you are ready and willing to pursue the matter may convince the driver to moderate his request.

18 For information about owning and driving an automobile in the People's Republic, see Laurence W. Bates and Andre T. Goldstein, "Sunday Drivers—All Week Long," *China Business Review* 16, no. 6 (November-December 1989): 36–39.

[19] Steven Bochner, "The Mediating Man and Cultural Diversity," in *Culture Learning: Concepts, Applications, and Research*, edited by Richard Brislin (Honolulu: University Press of Hawaii, 1977).

[20] Marcia Miller, "Reflections on Re-entry after Teaching in China," *Occasional Papers in Intercultural Learning* 14 (1988). Distributed by The AFS Center for the Study of Intercultural Learning, New York.

[21] Craig Storti, *The Art of Coming Home* (Yarmouth, ME: Intercultural Press, 1997).

Appendix A
Glossary of Chinese Terms

The purpose of this glossary is to enable you to pronounce in the Mandarin dialect all Chinese words and phrases appearing in the text. These are arranged alphabetically according to the pinyin transcription system of romanized spelling. Each word is followed by its approximate pronunciation using the equivalent English phonology and the appropriate pinyin tone graphs (absence of a tone graph indicates fifth, or neutral, tone). Also appearing are the location(s) in this book where the word or phrase is discussed (a chapter number followed by an *n* means that the word is discussed in that chapter's notes) and a brief explanation of its meaning and cultural implications.

A second appendix, "Chinese Titles and Forms of Address," lists the most common Chinese occupational titles.

For additional information regarding the pronunciation of pinyin and the appropriate use of the five tones of Mandarin, see any English-Mandarin dictionary or language-learning textbook.

Pinyin Transcription	Pronunciation Using English Phonology and Mandarin Tone Graphs	Location(s) in Text	Meaning in English and Implications in Chinese Culture
ama	āh māh	part II	Alternative for ayi often used in the southern provinces of China.
ayi	āh yée	part II, IIn	"Aunt." A pseudokinship term used by children (and their parents) for their caretakers and women of their mother's generation.
baba	bàh bah	chapter 3	"Father; daddy."
biaozhun	bēe-ow djŭn	part II	"Standard" or quality of a restaurant's meals. The biaozhun is expressed as price on a per capita basis and varies from city to city and from restaurant to restaurant.
biren	bèe rén	chapter 6	"My humble self." A word in classical Chinese, still occasionally used to show modesty.
bu hao	bòo hŏw	chapter 6	"Not good." Bu hao is used by the Chinese to ritually deny the validity of a compliment.
chi le ma?	chūr lay mah	chapter 3	"Have you eaten?" A form of greeting; rarely a genuine question.
danwei	dāhn wày	chapter 1; chapter 9; part II	"Work unit," that is, employing institution. A danwei has much more influence over a Chinese person than a U.S. employing institution has over an American.

Pinyin Transcription	Pronunciation Using English Phonology and Mandarin Tone Graphs	Location(s) in Text	Meaning in English and Implications in Chinese Culture
dengji	dūng jèe	part II	"Sign in." A system under which certain Chinese entering a hotel, dormitory, or apartment building occupied by foreigners must give information about themselves at the gate or in the lobby.
ganbu	gàhn boò	chapter 1n	"Cadre." A staff member of the Chinese government at all levels. Also used to refer to a white-collar worker or a leader in all walks of life.
ganqing	gǎhn chíng	chapter 7n	"Feelings; emotions; sentiments." The affective component of guanxi.
gege	gūh guh	chapter 1	"Elder brother."
gerenzhuyi	gùh rén djew yeè	chapter 7; part II	"Individualism" (literally, "one person doctrine"). Often used by the Chinese in a derogatory sense to imply selfishness.
guanxi	gwāhn shyee	chapter 7, 7n; chapter 9; part II	Not precisely translatable into English. Guanxi is often spoken of as something that links two people who have developed a relationship of mutual dependence.

Pinyin Transcription	Pronunciation Using English Phonology and Mandarin Tone Graphs	Location(s) in Text	Meaning in English and Implications in Chinese Culture
jiaoshu yüren	jēē-ow shòh yèw rén	chapter 8	"To teach book [and] to educate people," ideally the dual purposes of Chinese education. Jiaoshu refers narrowly to instruction. Yüren refers broadly to teaching humans how to live (yü means to nurture, rear) and thus connotes mentorship.
jiejie	jěe-eh jee-eh	chapter 1	"Elder sister."
kaolü	cǒw lèw	chapter 10	A phrase indicating that "We must give it more thought," or "We'll think this over further."
keqi	kùh chee	chapter 6	"Courteous; polite; civil." The implication of keqi is that self-deprecation plays a role in courteous or polite behavior.
lao	lǎow	chapter 2, 2n	"Old, senior." A prefix to the family name of a person older than oneself with whom one is on friendly terms.
laoshi	lǎow shur	chapter 2; chapter 8	"Teacher." A term of reverence for teachers at all levels, nursery school through university.
li	lěe	chapter 10, 10n	"Propriety, ritual politeness, decorum." More broadly, right conduct through maintaining one's place in the hierarchical order.

Pinyin Transcription	Pronunciation Using English Phonology and Mandarin Tone Graphs	Location(s) in Text	Meaning in English and Implications in Chinese Culture
liuban	lée-oo bàhn	part II	"Foreign student office." The university office handling the affairs of foreign students.
lüxingshe	lĕw shyíng shùh	part II	"Travel agency."
mafan ni	máh fahn neĕ	part II	"Excuse me" (literally, "troubling you"). A polite way to get the attention of a stranger.
maotai	máo tyé	part II	A strong and expensive Chinese liquor (produced in Maotai, Guizhou Province), often served at banquets to demonstrate the host's hospitality.
nali	nǎh lee	chapter 6	"Where?" Nali, nali? is used by the Chinese to ritually deny the validity of a compliment.
nán	náhn	part II	"Male." Most commonly seen on entrances to men's toilets.
nar qu ya?	nǎhr chòo yah	chapter 3	"Where are you going?" A form of greeting; rarely a genuine question.
ni hao	née hŏw	chapter 3	"Hello; hi; good day; greetings" (literally, "You are well"). A greeting used in a very wide range of social situations and at all times of day.

Pinyin Transcription	Pronunciation Using English Phonology and Mandarin Tone Graphs	Location(s) in Text	Meaning in English and Implications in Chinese Culture
ni hao ma?	née hǒw mah	chapter 3	"How are you? Are you well?" The interrogatory variation of ni hao, this greeting is received as a genuine question about well-being.
ni qu nar?	něe choò nǎhr	chapter 3	"Where are you going?" A variation of the greeting nar qu ya?
ni zao	né dsǒw	chapter 3	"Good morning" (literally, "You are early").
nin hao	nín hǒw	chapter 3	"Hello," etc. A variation of ni hao implying greater politeness. More frequently used by people in the Beijing area.
nü	něw	part II	"Female." Most commonly seen on entrances to women's toilets.
nüshi	něw shùr	chapter 2	"Ms., Madam." A suffix to the family name of an unmarried or married woman, as in Deng nüshi (Madam Deng).
pinyin	pīn yīn	introduction	"Phonetic transcriptions."
ren	rén	chapter 9	"Warmheartedness, benevolence, readiness to care for others," a personal quality valued by the Chinese in their leaders.
renao	rèh nòw	part II	"Lively; jolly; animated; exciting" (literally, "heat and noise").

Pinyin Transcription	Pronunciation Using English Phonology and Mandarin Tone Graphs	Location(s) in Text	Meaning in English and Implications in Chinese Culture
renminbi	rén mín bèe	part II, IIn	"People's currency," ordinary Chinese money.
shifu	shīh foo	chapter 2	"Master worker." A term used to address someone involved in a skill- or service-linked occupation. It need not be appended to his or her family name.
suihe	swéi heh	chapter 9	"Ready to blend in; blending into the situation." Going along with the group or the leader to maintain harmony.
taitai	tiè tie	chapter 2, 2n	"Mrs." A suffix not widely used in the People's Republic because married women do not take their husband's family name. Ignore suggestion of guidebooks and use nüshi instead.
tongzhi	tóng djùr	chapter 2	"Comrade." Not necessarily associated with the Communist party. A term used by the Chinese for addressing another Chinese who is a stranger, such as when asking for information on the street.
waiban	whỳ bahǹ	part II, IIn	"Foreign affairs office." The office of a danwei assigned to handle the affairs of foreign employees.

Pinyin Transcription	Pronunciation Using English Phonology and Mandarin Tone Graphs	Location(s) in Text	Meaning in English and Implications in Chinese Culture
wanshang hao	wǎhn shàhng hǒw	chapter 3	"Good evening." Understood but not widely used in the PRC.
wushui	wǒo shwày	chapter 5, 5n; chapter 8	"Nap after lunch; rest in the afternoon."
xiansheng	shyēē-an shung	chapter 2	"Mr." A suffix to the family name of a man, as in Chen xiansheng (Mr. Chen).
xiao	shyěe-ow	chapter 2, 2n	"Young, junior." A prefix to the family name of a person younger than oneself with whom one is on friendly terms.
xiaojie	shyée-ow jěe-eh	chapter 2	"Miss." A suffix to the family name of a young, unmarried woman, as in Zhou xiaojie (Miss Zhou). Also used to get the attention of a young woman who is a waitress or shop attendant; in this case, it need not be appended to her family name.
xie xie	shyeè-eh shyee-eh	part IIn	"Thank you."
yinsi	yǐn sūh	chapter 5	"Privacy." This term more accurately means "hidden private affairs" and may carry the connotation of shady dealing and deceptive secrecy.
youyi	yǒh yeè	chapter 9	"Friendship." Toasts are sometimes made to youyi during banquets.

Pinyin Transcription	Pronunciation Using English Phonology and Mandarin Tone Graphs	Location(s) in Text	Meaning in English and Implications in Chinese Culture
yüren	yèw rén	chapter 8	See jiaoshu yüren.
zaijian	dsaì jeè-en	chapter 3	"Good-bye" (literally, "again to see").
zao	dsǒw	chapter 3	"Good morning." Variation of ni zao.
zaoshang hao	dsǒw shàhng hǒw	chapter 3	"Good morning." Understood but not widely used in the PRC.

Appendix B
Chinese Titles and Forms of Address

Following are common Chinese occupation titles. Such titles are used with great frequency in the People's Republic of China. They are spoken and written after the family name of the individual in question. For additional information about the use of occupational titles, see chapter 2.

Pinyin Transcription	Pronunciation Using English Phonology and Mandarin Tone Graphs	Meaning in English
Government		
buzhang	boò djăhng	minister
chuzhang	choò djăhng	director (of a subdepartment)
fu buzhang	foò boò djăhng	vice minister
fu zongli	foò dsóng lěe	vice premier
ganbu	gàhn boò	cadre (see chapter 1, note 4)
juzhang	jóo djăhng	director (of a bureau)
kezhang	kūh djăhng	section head
shengzhang	shúng djăhng	governor
shizhang	shùr djăhng	mayor
sizhang	sūh djăhng	director (of a department)
zongli	dsóng lěe	premier
Business and Industry		
changzhang	cháng djăhng	factory manager or director
chejian zhuren	chūh jēē-an djěw rèn	workshop foreman
gongchengshi	gōng chúng shūr	engineer
jingli	jīng lěe	manager
zong gong	djǒng gōng	short for zong gongchengshi
zong gongchengshi	djǒng gōng chúng shūr	engineer-in-chief
zong jingli	djǒng jīng lěe	general manager

Pinyin Transcription	Pronunciation Using English Phonology and Mandarin Tone Graphs	Meaning in English
Education (Universities)		
jiaoshou	jeè-ow shòh	professor
jiaoyanshi zhuren	jeè-ow yáhn shūr djěw rèn	head of a teaching and research group
shi zhuren	shūr djěw rèn	short for jiaoyanshi zhuren
xiaozhang	shyeè-ow djǎhng	president or chancellor
xi zhuren	shyeè djěw rèn	department chairperson
Miscellaneous Occupational Titles		
bianji	bēē-en jée	editor
jiangjun	geè-ahng jōōn	military commander; general
shuji	shōō jeè	party secretary
yisheng	yēē shūng	medical doctor
zhuren	djěw rèn	director
zhuxi	djěw shyée	chairman (of a committee)

Recommended Readings

The following books are outstanding in their portrayal of the cultural characteristics and the social and communicative patterns of the Chinese from the People's Republic of China.

Bond, Michael Harris. *Beyond the Chinese Face: Insights from Psychology*. Hong Kong: Oxford University Press, 1991. 125 pages.

Although this summary volume was originally meant to complement Bond's previous work, *The Psychology of the Chinese People* (see below), it stands alone as a good short introduction to Chinese social, educational, and bureaucratic patterns. Particularly of use to businesspeople is the chapter "Chinese Organizational Life," where topics ranging from leadership to decision making are discussed. Bond's perspective on the workplace is occasionally distorted by his academic approach—but his breadth and open-mindedness compensate nicely in most cases. For educators, Bond summarizes Chinese learning styles and patterns of thinking in the chapter "How Chinese Think."

Bond, Michael Harris, ed. *The Psychology of the Chinese People*. Hong Kong: Oxford University Press, 1986. 354 pages.

Michael Harris Bond is the leading Western scholar focusing on the psychology and sociology of the Chinese. In this and other works he has shown his determination to understand the Chinese from a Sinocentric, not a Western, perspective. Most of the eight other contributing scholars have an ethnic Chinese background, and all, like Bond, are based in Hong Kong or Taiwan. Chapter titles include "Chinese Patterns of Socialization," "Chinese Personality and Its Change," and "The Psychology of Chinese Organizational Behavior." Included is an exhaustive bibliography in which Chinese scholars are heavily represented. This book is a "must read" for anyone seriously committed to understanding the values and culture of the PRC.

de Keijzer, Arne J. *China: Business Strategies for the '90s.* Berkeley, CA: Pacific View Press, 1992. 279 pages.

As the author of two previous books on China, *The China Guidebook* and *The China Business Handbook*, Arne J. de Keijzer brings to this volume many years of China trade and consulting experience. Although certain portions of this work are already out-of-date, it is well researched and continues to provide useful management information relevant to operating a business in China. Numerous checklists as well as executive summaries of case studies and strategic concepts make it accessible to businesspeople whose reading time is limited. (The case studies explore the experiences of companies from Europe, Japan, Hong Kong, Canada, and the United States.) Several pages near the end of the book provide annotated criteria for successful China ventures.

Eisenberg, David. *Encounters with Qi: Exploring Chinese Medicine.* New York: W. W. Norton, 1995. 260 pages.

David Eisenberg learned acupuncture, massage, and herbal techniques as the first U.S. medical exchange student to the People's Republic of China, where he worked beside his teachers in Chinese clinics. He has continued to investigate Chinese medicine as a clinical research fellow at Harvard Medical School. Eisenberg's account is useful both for its inside look at the ancient medical techniques of the *Qi* (pronounced chee) and for its depiction of daily life and work in Chinese medical facilities. He also discusses the concept of mental illness in China and devotes much attention to the amazing physical feats of the Qi Gong masters. *Encounters with* Qi is balanced and fascinating.

Gao, Ge, and Stella Ting-Toomey. *Communicating Effectively with the Chinese*. Thousand Oaks, CA: Sage, 1998. 109 pages.
   This little gem of a book is a well-informed and insightful discussion of the characteristics of Chinese communication. Although authored by two academics, it will be easily understandable by businesspeople and other nonacademics; the text itself is only ninety-three pages long. Chinese terms and quotes in English are followed by Chinese characters. Examples of everyday talk are deconstructed to reveal subtly contrasting cultural assumptions. The final chapter analyzes why miscommunication between Chinese and North Americans takes place ("polite versus impolite," "hesitant versus assertive," and "self-effacing versus self-enhancing" are among the categories) and offers suggestions to both Chinese and North Americans for improving their communication with each other.

Holm, Bill. *Coming Home Crazy: An Alphabet of China Essays*. Minneapolis: Milkweed Editions, 1990. 251 pages.
   An accomplished author and musician, this professor from Minnesota spins great yarns of the life of one foreigner in the People's Republic of China. Humor and spicy wording make this a favorite read, covering topics from the usefulness of a Swiss army knife to coping with Chinese bureaucracy. Most of Holm's adventures take place in the interior cities of China such as Xi'an and Chengdu, so foreigners familiar with the coastal cities might view Holm's experiences—mistakenly—as outdated or quaint. The true gift of this book, though, is its thoughtful approach to cultural relativity.

Hsu, Francis L. K. *Americans and Chinese: Passage to Differences*, 3d ed. Honolulu: The University Press of Hawaii, 1981. 534 pages.

The late Francis L. K. Hsu was born in China, did graduate work in the United Kingdom and the United States, carried out fieldwork in China, and was a professor of anthropology in the United States. His numerous writings have focused on the differences between China and the United States from the point of view of psychological anthropology; see the collection of his articles entitled *Rugged Individualism Reconsidered* (Knoxville: University of Tennessee Press, 1983). Some of Hsu's views are questionable—for example, he overstates adult Americans' physical and emotional separation from their parents, and his views on sexual repression in the United States are now outdated—but his works nevertheless are an outstanding attempt to analyze and compare the values and behavior of Americans and Chinese.

Jones, Stephanie. *Managing in China: An Executive Survival Guide*. Singapore: Butterworth-Heinemann Asia, 1997. 260 pages.

Based on the author's experiences as an expatriate in Shanghai and on her interviews with many other Western and overseas Chinese expatriates working for multinational firms, *Managing in China* is a useful guide for those who want to succeed in business as well as cope well with daily life in China. The guidelines it offers are sensible and balanced and are amplified by expatriate stories and excerpts from Chinese history and folklore. Unique in showing how Western- and Chinese-heritage expats experience today's China differently, this is a readable snapshot of how those who have gone before were able to survive and prosper.

Li, Victor H. *Law without Lawyers: A Comparative View of Law in China and the United States*. Boulder, CO: Westview Press, 1978. 102 pages.

Victor H. Li, a specialist in Chinese law, became president of the East-West Center in Honolulu in 1981. Li's title refers to the fact that in the mid-1970s, there was in the United States approximately one lawyer for every 500 people while in China there was approximately one lawyer for every 230,000 people. Li examines the underlying cultural and social differences that make this stark discrepancy a reality. He is particularly good at drawing comparisons between the American and Chinese ways of controlling conduct and defining deviance. Even though the passage of time has rendered out-of-date many of its details regarding Chinese legal practice, this book continues to provide valuable insight into historical forces and basic values that shape daily life in both China and the United States.

Macleod, Roderick. *China, Inc.: How to Do Business with the Chinese*. New York: Bantam Books, 1988. 224 pages.

Macleod was the first foreign accountant to set up shop in China after the Cultural Revolution and later became the founder and CEO of two Chinese-American joint ventures. He learned about doing business in China by profiting from his own mistakes as well as those of other Westerners who had come to China with high hopes but no cultural sensitivity. His title, *China, Inc.*, is intended to convey the extent to which business in China is controlled by the government. But the real value of his book lies in the ten "Businessmen's Horror Stories" he tells about the cultural errors made by foreigners in China and in his discussions of typical business problems—some Chinese in origin, some Western in origin, some common to both sides. This book has a breezy style that makes for easy reading.

Pratt, Daniel D. "Conceptions of Self Within China and the United States: Contrasting Foundations for Adult Education." *International Journal of Intercultural Relations* 15, no. 3 (1991): 285–310.

If you are committed to understanding the differences between U.S. and Chinese conceptions of self, this short journal article is well worth the effort to acquire. Pratt insightfully probes and incisively describes the wellsprings of identity in the two cultures, providing details about the contrast we often refer to simply as "individualism" versus "collectivism." For those interested in adult education and corporate training issues across the Chinese-U.S. cultural divide, this article is indispensable.

Pye, Lucian W. *Chinese Negotiating Style: Commercial Approaches and Cultural Principles*. Rev. ed. New York: Quorum Books, 1992. 119 pages.

Lucian W. Pye, a political psychologist and leading American authority on Asian politics, is a professor at Massachusetts Institute of Technology and a consultant to the Rand Corporation. His Chinese commercial negotiating style was developed from interviews with American and other foreign businesspeople operating in China and is intended primarily for those who will be doing business there. Pye not only describes in detail all aspects of negotiations with the Chinese but also examines emotional and other sources of the Chinese negotiating style. This book is a "must read" for anyone seriously committed to understanding the values and culture of the PRC.

Seligman, Scott D. *Dealing with the Chinese: A Practical Guide to Business Etiquette in the People's Republic Today*. New York: Warner Books, 1989. 213 pages. Rev. ed. forthcoming 1999.

Formerly a staff member at the National Council for U. S.-China Trade as well as a founding member of the American Chamber of Commerce in Beijing, Scott D. Seligman has written a book that is packed with useful information. Its physical size as well as its clearly delineated internal structure makes it an excellent handbook for Americans who are doing business in China. Among the chapter titles are "The Business Meeting," "Relationships with Foreigners," and "Getting Things Done in China." One unusual but welcome feature is a section (in chapter 3) on Chinese nonverbal communication. Another is a chapter entitled "Hosting the Chinese," in which Seligman gives detailed advice to people in the United States who are receiving Chinese delegations.

Seybolt. Peter J. *Through Chinese Eyes: Revolution and Transformation*. Rev. ed. New York: Center for International Training and Education, 1988. 280 pages.

The stated goal of this collection is to present a Chinese view of China and the world. Almost everything in this volume was written by Chinese; included are autobiography, fiction, poetry, newspaper articles, and historical documents. As the foreword states, "*Through Chinese Eyes* does not try to explain China but to show it; it does not offer 'expert' analysis [but rather] attempts to recreate the reality of everyday life as experienced by the Chinese." Part I depicts the social revolution brought about by the Communist party and includes material on recent changes in family life, religion, women's roles, and politics. Part II explores debates within China over economic development, health care, population growth, the proper path for socialism, and other issues; it ends with a section on the Chinese-American experience. Teacher's manuals suitable for high school and college courses are available for Parts I and II.

Thurston, Anne F. *China Bound: A Guide to Academic Life and Work in the PRC*. Rev. ed. Washington, DC: National Academy Press, 1994. 252 pages.

China Bound is the definitive guide for scholars, educators, teachers, and students who are or will be living and working in China. It discusses opportunities for and realities of research, study, and teaching in China; preparations that one should make before departing; the process of settling in after arriving; services that are available to the expatriate; and the process of departing. Seventeen appendices offer additional valuable information.

Yang, Mayfair Mei-hui. *Gifts, Favors and Banquets: The Art of Social Relationships in China*. Ithaca: Cornell University Press, 1994. 370 pages.

Based on extensive fieldwork, Yang's book describes how the "gift economy" of *guanxi* operates in the socialist market economy of the People's Republic of China. Her studies show how practicing the art of guanxi provides Chinese people with a foundation for improving their lot and accomplishing myriad tasks, from getting favorable job assignments to obtaining desirable housing. Although the concept and practice of building guanxi has deep roots in traditional Chinese culture, Yang shows how this art has gained special impetus in China, with people honing specific skills in circumventing obstacles presented by its unique economy. This is a sound academic study but might be unwieldy for the business reader.

China Books and Periodicals, a publishing and book distribution company, carries a wide range of books about China and specializes in manuals and tapes for learning Mandarin and other dialects. Ask to be put on its catalogue mailing list. Contact China Books and Periodicals, 2929 24th Street, San Francisco, CA 94110; telephone: 415-282-2994; fax: 415-282-0994; Website: http://www.chinabooks.com

Another source of English-language books about China is the China International Book Trading Corporation, which publishes a small, partially annotated catalogue entitled *Books from China*, covering books on a wide range of topics from numerous Chinese publishers. Contact China International Book Trading Corporation, P.O. Box 399, Beijing 100044, People's Republic of China; telephone: 011-86-10-6841-4284; fax: 011-86-10-6841-2023.